D1256992

Business Principles of Landscape Contracting

Steven M. Cohan
University of Maryland

PROPERTY OF
SENECA COLLEGE
LIBRARIES
KING CAMPUS

PEARSON
Prentice
Hall

Upper Saddle River, New Jersey
Columbus, Ohio

Library of Congress Cataloging-in-Publication Data

Cohan, Steven M.
  Business principles of landscape contracting / Steven M. Cohan.
    p. cm.
  Includes index.
  ISBN 0-13-111678-9 (paperback)
    1. Landscape contracting. I. Title.

SB472.55.C64 2006
712'.068'1—dc22

2005043020

Executive Editor: Debbie Yarnell
Assistant Editor: Maria Rego
Production Editor: Alexandrina Benedicto Wolf
Production Liaison: Carlisle Publishers Services
Design Coordinator: Diane Ernsberger
Cover Designer: Thomas Mack
Cover Photo: The Brickman Group
Production Manager: Matt Ottenweller
Marketing Manager: Jimmy Stephens

This book was set in Times Roman by Carlisle Communications, Ltd., and was printed and bound by R.R. Donnelley & Sons Company. The cover was printed by Phoenix Color Corp.

Copyright © 2006 by Pearson Education, Inc., Upper Saddle River, New Jersey 07458. Pearson Prentice Hall. All rights reserved. Printed in the United States of America. This publication is protected by Copyright and permission should be obtained from the publisher prior to any prohibited reproduction, storage in a retrieval system, or transmission in any form or by any means, electronic, mechanical, photocopying, recording, or likewise. For information regarding permission(s), write to: Rights and Permissions Department.

Pearson Prentice Hall™ is a trademark of Pearson Education, Inc.
Pearson® is a registered trademark of Pearson plc
Prentice Hall® is a registered trademark of Pearson Education, Inc.

Pearson Education Ltd.
Pearson Education Singapore, Pte. Ltd.
Pearson Education Canada, Ltd.
Person Education–Japan

Pearson Education Australia PTY, Limited
Pearson Education North Asia Ltd.
Pearson Educación de Mexico, S.A. de C.V.
Pearson Education Malaysia, Ptd. Ltd.

10 9 8 7 6 5 4 3 2 1
ISBN: 0-13-111678-9

To my wife, Diane, and sons Todd and Brad,
for their patience and support throughout the development of the manuscript,
and to the many individuals in the academic and landscape industry communities
whose reviews and information enhanced the pedagogy and credibility of the manuscript.

Preface

After five years of gathering information from landscape trade association publications and trade journals for my course in "Commercial Principles of Landscape Management," I began the arduous task of writing this book. I wanted to have all the information I needed under one cover and in a pedagogical style that my students could comprehend. This is the first textbook that essentially translates business principles into a language that can be understood by college students enrolled in landscape management and landscape contracting programs. In contrast to the manual, how-to style of trade publications and articles, *Business Principles of Landscape Contracting* emphasizes business principles and their applications to the landscape industry.

The landscape contracting industry is comprised of companies ranging in sales from the hundreds of thousands to over a billion dollars. The challenge these companies face is maximizing production efficiency while maintaining quality production standards. Regardless of their sales volume, the formula for a company's financial success is the same: **lower costs + productivity efficiency = profitability.** This formula can only be implemented if the company identifies, and most importantly measures, each of its production components. This point is articulated in the management philosophy of The Brickman Group, Ltd., "With passion we strive to understand and measure where we are."

This textbook provides a comprehensive description of the financial components that enable a company to measure its bottom-line profitability. The chapters are sequenced in a toolbox fashion, filling the financial management box with essential tools for building a database, a budget, a pricing structure, and an accounting system capable of generating timely reports on the current financial status of the company and its profit centers.

Since the landscape industry is service oriented, the human element could not be ignored. It's people, not machines, who produce the end product for all landscape companies. Therefore, chapters are devoted to personnel management, professional development, employee productivity, and leadership. The latter is critical to the development and retention of a company's human assets. Integral to the discussion of employee retention is company culture, which is defined and exemplified by both landscape companies and other types of businesses.

This is not a textbook of theory but rather one of practice. Figures and text contain information that have been researched directly from design/build and landscape maintenance companies. Knowledge application exercises at the end of each chapter reinforce the content and its significance to the industry. The knowledge gleaned from the text will benefit students whose career goals include entrepreneurship or management positions within the landscape industry.

ACKNOWLEDGMENTS

Gratitude is extended to the plethora of industry individuals who provided "real-life" business scenarios for the topics discussed throughout the book. Their advice and critiques were invaluable in the evolvement of the text and in establishing its credibility.

I'd like to specifically acknowledge the following individuals whose reviews and contributions had a significant impact on the development of this textbook:

All Season Care
Richard Redfern

American Mortgage
Marc Purvis

Ariens
Daniel Ariens
Carol Dilger

Black & Decker
Brad Cohan

Bozzuto Landscaping
Thomas Davis
Randy Abshier
Matthew Glyder

The Brickman Group, Ltd.
Bruce Hunt
Jeffrey Topley
Joseph Ketterer

Chapel Valley Landscape Co.
J. Landon Reeve IV
Terri Feldhaus
Bryan Arnold
Edward Delaha
Jennifer Buck
Samuel Bettien

Control Environmental Services, Inc.
Michael Aschenbrenner

Garden Gate Landscape
Charles Bowers
Daniel Law

JP Horizons
James Paluch

Kinnucan Co.
Robert Kinnucan

Kraft Associates/ODA Inc.
Joel McFadden

McHale Landscape
Kevin McHale
Phillip Kelly
Sally Barker
Hans Blienerger

Ruppert Companies
Craig Ruppert
Chris Davitt
Jay Long

TruGreen LandCare
Larry Leon
Seven Von Essen
Ron Anduray

My appreciation is further extended to academic colleagues whose insight and pedagogical perspectives have been incorporated into the manuscript.

Brigham Young University
Philip Allen

Columbus State Community College
Richard Ansley
Steven O'Neal

California State Polytechnic University
Steven Angley
Dr. Fred Roth

Hinds Community College
Martha Hill

Illinois Central College
Randey Wall

Pennsylvania State University
Daniel Stearns

University of Maryland
Dennis Nola
Dr. Christopher Walsh
Dr. Richard Weismiller

University of Tennessee
Gary Menendez

I would also like to thank the following reviewers for their invaluable feedback: Michael Davidsohn, University of Massachusetts-Amherst; Greg Davis, Kansas State University; Dee Johnson, Sandhills Community College; Kevin McHale, University of Maryland; Eddie Dean Seagle, Abraham Baldwin Agricultural College; and Dan T. Stearns, Penn State.

Additional Resources

ONLINE SUPPLEMENTS ACCOMPANY THE TEXT

An online Instructor's Manual and TestGen are also available to instructors through the Cohan catalog page at **www. prenhall.com**. Instructors can search for a text by author, title, ISBN, or by selecting the appropriate discipline from the pull down menu at the top of the catalog home page. To access supplementary materials online, instructors need to request an instructor access code. Go to **www.prenhall.com**, click the **Instructor Resource Center** link, and then click **Register Today** for an instructor access code. Within 48 hours after registering you will receive a confirming e-mail including an instructor access code. Once you have received your code, go to the site and log on for full instructions on downloading the materials you wish to use.

AGRICULTURE SUPERSITE

This site is a free on-line resource center for both students and instructors in the Agricultural field. Located at **http://www.prenhall.com/agsite**, students will find additional study questions, job search links, photo galleries, PowerPoints, The New York Times eThemes archive, and other agricultural-related links.

Instructors will find a complete listing of Prentice Hall's agriculture titles, as well as instructor supplements supporting Prentice Hall Agriculture textbooks available for immediate download. Please contact your Prentice Hall sales representative for password information.

"THE NEW YORK TIMES" THEMES OF THE TIMES FOR AGRICULTURE

Taken directly from the pages of *The New York Times*, these carefully edited collections of articles offer students insight into the hottest issues facing the industry today. These free supplements can be packaged along with the text.

AGRIBOOKS: A CUSTOM PUBLISHING PROGRAM FOR AGRICULTURE

Just can't find the textbook that fits *your* class? Here is your chance to create your own ideal book by mixing and matching chapters from Prentice Hall's agriculture textbooks. Up to 20% of your custom book can be your own writing or come from outside sources. Visit us at: **http://www.prenhall.com/agribooks**.

Contents

Chapter 4

Estimating 51

Chapter 5

Financial Management 67

Chapter 6

Financial Ratios 87

Chapter 7

Software Applications   103

Chapter 8

Managing Human Assets   113

Chapter 9

Productivity Basics   133

Structuring for Accountability

CHAPTER OBJECTIVES

To gain an understanding of:

1. Accounting methods
   a. Distinctions
   b. Function
   c. Applications

2. Accounting system infrastructure
   a. Chart of accounts
      1. Guidelines
      2. Classification
      3. Terminology
      4. Accountability

We are all structured for financial accountability. Our personal budget allocates disbursements of our monthly income to specific categories, such as rent, utilities, mortgage, clothing, entertainment, and so on. Recording these disbursements in the checkbook represents one facet of accounting, a process that categorizes and summarizes recorded transactions. The checkbook serves as a recording device but does not summarize and categorize the financial entries. We can accomplish the balance of the accounting process either by employing an accounting software program or by manually categorizing transactions in a ledger. A **ledger** is an accounting book that summarizes and categorizes information from individual accounts into single locations. Information from individual accounts is posted (recorded) on a weekly or monthly basis. Ledgers enable managers to easily access this summarized information. Accounting software programs make electronic postings into computerized ledgers whenever journal entries are made in individual accounts. An **accounting system** processes the recorded information into financial statements. These statements provide an assessment of our current financial status and details pertaining to all of the individual financial transactions. We can get breakdowns of our expenses, for example, what we spent for entertainment, automobile, clothing, insurance, and so on. How effectively we manage our accounting system and

ledger
an accounting book that summarizes and categorizes information from individual accounts into single accounts.

accounting system
processes the recorded information into financial statements.

utilize it to make our financial decisions determines whether we will be able to meet our financial obligations.

PURCHASE ORDER LEDGER

Date	P.O. #	Ordered By	For Dept.	Vendor	Job Name	Materials	Inv. #	Yard	Dollars Const.	$ Irrigation Lights	Date Expected

cash flow
represents the balance between revenue and expenses during a period of time.

positive cash flow
when revenue exceeds expenses.

negative cash flow
when expenses exceed cash flow within a specific period of time.

expenses
all the costs associated with the sales of goods and services and those associated with business operations.

maximizing profit
achieved with an accounting system that enables management to monitor the financial status of the company on a daily basis.

In the business world, meeting financial obligations and attaining profit goals requires astute management of two primary components, cash flow and expenses. **Cash flow** represents the amount of revenue (income) a company receives from the sale of goods and services in relation to its expenses. It can be thought of in terms of the balance between income and expenses. **Positive cash flow** is when the amount of revenue exceeds the amount of expenses, and **negative cash flow** is when expenses exceed revenue within a specific time period. **Expenses** are all the costs associated with the sales of goods and services and those costs associated with business operations, for example, for utilities. The successful management of these components cannot occur without a comprehensive accounting system. This system is the source of all the financial information that is derived from recorded transactions. These transactions include all revenue (income) from the sales of goods and services and disbursements associated with the sales and business operations.

Maximizing profit can only be achieved with an accounting system that enables management to monitor the financial status of the company on a daily basis. Unlike monthly financial statements, which are historical documents, daily financial reports provide current information that enables management to identify where adjustments need to be made to meet budget figures. Charlie Bowers, CEO of Garden Gate Landscaping, Inc., summarized the value of such an accounting system:

> ■ "By being able to see the future and the present earlier, you can be proactive rather than reactive when looking at historical financial statements." ■

An example of being proactive would be directing more effort into securing sales in specific profit centers based upon an assessment of actual versus budgeted sales figures. Reviewing current financial data will also enable adjustments to be made in overhead and direct expenses if their percentages are exceeding projections. **Overhead expenses** are those that support the sales of goods and services such as administrative expenses and equipment maintenance. **Direct expenses** are those associated with sales, such as labor and materials.

overhead expenses
are those that support the sales of goods and services such as administrative expenses and equipment maintenance.

direct expenses
are associated with job production, such as labor and materials.

Once the financial information is categorized and summarized, reports and statements can be generated to provide an analysis of the current financial health of the business. Integrated software programs adapted to the Green Industry enable immediate access to reports on any facet of the business with the touch of a key. Managers may access current job cost analyses, a division's current sales and profits against budgeted projections, hardscape inventory, or any other information that has been documented in the system. Some landscape companies provide their managers with handheld computers for accessing the system in the field. Managers utilize this technology to input and download client and job data.

Management depends on current financial information to make decisions on operational procedures, pricing, hiring, equipment purchasing, acquisitions, marketing, and other business activities that require financial transactions. Accounting provides the communication link between management and the business finances. A profile of this communication link is illustrated in Figure 1-1. The output provides management

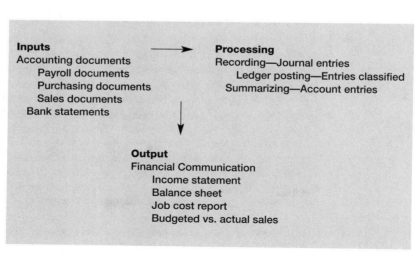

Figure 1-1 Accounting System Profile

with information that will influence decisions on current production and operations as well as future growth and development.

■ Accounting Methods

cash basis method
of accounting: records revenue only when payments are received and expenses only when checks are issued.

revenue
is the dollar value of materials and services sold.

accounts receivable
represents total monies owed to a company by its clients.

accounts payable
represents total monies owed by a company for job materials.

profit
is the amount of money left after a company has met its current financial obligations.

inventory
purchased materials that are not currently assigned to specific jobs.

assets
any items that have monetary value.

The primary function of an accounting method is to provide management with the most accurate current status of profitability. The different accounting methods are cash basis and accrual basis. Two variations of the accrual method are billings and percentage of completion.

The **cash basis method** of accounting records **revenue** which is the dollar value of materials and services sold, only when payments are received and records expenses only when checks are issued, similar to a checking account. Therefore it does not reflect the current status of **accounts receivable,** which represents total monies owed to the company by clients or general contractors, or **accounts payable,** which represents total monies owed by the company for job materials. Accounting on this basis inaccurately reflects **profit,** which is the amount of money left after a company has met its current financial obligations.

Inventory, which is purchased materials that are not currently assigned to a specific job (such as boulders, trees, mulch, etc.), is recorded as an expense in cash basis accounting, rather than as an **asset,** which is any item that has monetary value. This assessment is erroneous, since inventory items will ultimately be assigned to contracted projects and will contribute to the total profit of the job. A landscape company can increase its profit by purchasing items at quantity discounts (trees and shrubs, fertilizers, hardscape materials like boulders and fieldstone) and maintaining an inventory to fulfill its seasonal needs. An inventory also can contribute to job cost savings by having items readily available for transport to the job site.

Because of the negatives of cash basis accounting, you may be wondering why a company would use this method. As noted in Figure 1-2, it is a simple system and

Advantages:
1. Simple to use.
2. Offers tax advantage since income can be changed from one financial period to another by regulating collections and expense disbursements.
3. Income tax is paid only on the actual money received.

Disadvantages:
1. Financial statements misrepresent the current financial status and therefore are useless as a basis for management decisions.
2. Most lending institutions will not issue credit based upon financial statements generated from cash-based accounting systems.

Figure 1-2 Cash Basis Accounting

Source: Designing Your Accounting System, by Ross/Payne & Associates, Inc., Professional Landcare Network, Herndon, VA.

therefore can be implemented easily. It also offers tax advantages since income tax is paid only on the revenue received rather than on the total revenue earned. A company's billing schedule can also control the amount of income tax that will be paid within a financial period, according to when the payments are received. Do these tax advantages outweigh the disadvantages of not having an accurate assessment of the company's current financial status? The answer is a resounding no and will be further reinforced in subsequent chapters.

Figure 1-3 illustrates how profit can be distorted by the cash basis method of accounting. The $30,000 differential in actual income will be received eventually, but it will be recorded in another financial period. Since overhead expenses are calculated as a percentage of total revenue, this figure is lower with cash basis accounting. In reality, the overhead expenses are based on the percentage of the total income figure. Again, the balance of overhead expenses will be recorded in another financial period.

As previously stated, revenue is only recorded as it is received and expenses as they are paid. Therefore, the cash basis method of accounting never truly reflects a company's income and expenses in a financial period. The same would hold true on individual jobs in which the dollar value of the job and its related expenses would only be reflected as revenue received and expenses paid.

accrual method
of accounting: cumulative, adding income based on billings and expenses based on receipt of invoices.

invoices
bills issued by vendors for purchase of plants and materials.

billings basis
records sales with each invoice issued and expenses with each vendor invoice received.

The **accrual method** of accounting, in contrast to the cash basis, is cumulative, adding income and expenses as clients are billed and invoices are received. **Invoices** are bills issued by vendors for purchases of plants and materials. Two variations of these systems are the billings basis and the percentage of completion basis. The **billings basis** (Figure 1-4) records sales with each invoice that is issued and expenses with each vendor invoice that is received. The fact that payments have not been received or that invoices have not been paid are not relevant to this accounting method. Its accuracy, in terms of reflecting profitability, is contingent upon expenses and revenue being accounted for in the same period. If the accounting department is a few weeks behind in posting billings and invoices, generated financial reports will be inaccurate.

The billings basis of accounting is more effectively employed with landscape maintenance contracts. The revenue associated with these contracts is prorated over twelve months. The monthly invoices (billings) are generated with the same dollar amount

January 1–March 31, 2004				
Actual			**Cash Basis Accounting**	
Sales Revenue	$210,000		Revenue Received	$180,000
Direct Job Costs				
Material	63,000		Materials—paid	51,000
Labor	42,000		Labor expenses—paid	42,000
Total Direct Costs	105,000		Total Direct Costs	96,000
Gross Profit Margin	105,000		Gross Profit Margin	84,000
Overhead	63,000		Overhead	54,000
Net Profit	42,000		Net Profit	30,000

Figure 1-3 Distorted Financial Perspective from Cash Basis Accounting

Advantages:

1. Simple to use.

2. Accurate if job billing is timely.

3. Tax liability may be designated for specific periods based upon when job invoices are issued.

4. Effective method for short-term installation jobs, which can be completed and invoiced in the same period, and for maintenance contracts.

Disadvantages:

1. Long-term installation jobs, which extend over several accounting periods, can result in distorted financial figures.

2. If receivables are not collected promptly, the company may pay taxes on uncollected income.

Figure 1-4   Billings Basis of Accounting

Source: Designing Your Accounting System, by Ross/Payne & Associates, Inc., Professional Landcare Network, Herndon, VA.

regardless of the services rendered during that period. Maintenance clients prefer this form of billing since it facilitates their budgeting process by assessing a fixed monthly amount for landscape services. Landscape maintenance companies are equally satisfied with the system since it provides a fixed amount of cash flow on a monthly basis. Costs associated with the monthly services (labor and materials) are posted as they are incurred (as vendor invoices are received). This method is also applicable for short-term installation/construction jobs that are completed within a financial period.

Accounting systems use financial periods to summarize all transactions. The reason this method is not practical for long-term installation/construction jobs is because they extend over several financial periods. Four of these periods comprise a company's financial or fiscal year.

The accuracy of the billings basis is contingent upon the company's billing schedule, since income is only posted when invoices are issued. Any delayed billing will distort the actual income for a period and thus the company's profit status. The timeliness of billing is equally important on an individual job basis to accurately reflect the job's profit status. In regard to tax liability, a company may pay taxes on uncollected income, since income is recorded based on billings. This situation can be avoided with stringent control over accounts receivable.

percentage of completion basis

accounts for the income and expenses associated with a percentage of job completion.

The most reliable of the accrual methods for long-term installation/construction contracts is the **percentage of completion basis.** This method is particularly adaptable to the commercial contracting business because it eliminates the inaccuracies associated with timing differences in billings and vendor invoices. The percentage of completion basis accounts for the income and expenses associated with percentage of job completion (e.g., 70%). Billing is submitted to the general contractor, generally on a monthly basis, for payment of services and materials completed to date. This method provides an up-to-date status of the revenue earned and costs incurred throughout the

Advantages:

1. Provides the most accurate financial profile for installation/construction contracts.

2. Allows ample time for tax planning because percentage of completion calculates tax exposure based on completed work.

Disadvantages:

1. It requires an accurate method for determining percentage of job completion.

2. Retainage monies are calculated into revenue even though they will not be received until a later date.

3. This method provides no flexibility for the deferral of income taxes.

Figure 1-5 Percentage of Completion Basis of Accounting

Source: Designing Your Accounting System, by Ross/Payne & Associates, Inc., Professional Landcare Network, Herndon, VA.

duration of the contract. Upon completion of the entire job, a composite of revenue and costs reported to date will indicate the profit status of the job.

The primary problem associated with the percentage of completion method is that there isn't a standardized technique for assessing the percentage of completion of a job. Therefore, this method is only as accurate as the contractor's method of determining the percentage of completion. However, most professional accountants are in agreement that the percentage of completion method is the most accurate for landscape construction companies.

retainage monies

retained by the client pending satisfactory completion of the job.

One of the disadvantages of this accounting method, noted in Figure 1-5, is the inclusion of retainage monies in the revenue calculation. **Retainage monies** are those that are retained by the client pending satisfactory completion of the job. Retainage is calculated as a percentage of the total contract price (generally equating to 10% of the total contract price). Since retainage is not paid immediately upon job completion, it is not a component of the revenue received. In essence, it can be considered as part of accounts receivable.

There are advantages and disadvantages to each accounting system: cash, billing, and percentage of completion. Landscape contactors use the billing basis for their maintenance clients and short-term plant installation jobs. Landscape construction and design/build companies that engage in long-term commercial contracts most often use the percentage of completion basis of accounting.

■ Chart of Accounts

chart of accounts

comprises the database from which the accounting system generates financial reports.

The **chart of accounts** (Figure 1-6) comprises the database from which the accounting system generates financial reports for the business. It provides a list of accounts to categorize all expenses and income associated with the operation of a business. Each account is assigned either an alphabetic or a numeric code to enable

1. Develop the chart of accounts according to the nature of the business and the desired financial information.
2. Establish a format that can be expanded or adjusted based upon a company's growth and information needs.
3. Make sure accounts clearly define costs and provide pertinent information required by management.
4. Make it concise and user friendly to enhance ease of implementation.

Figure 1-6 Chart of Accounts Guidelines

classification and access for financial analyses. The information that is categorized essentially becomes a reference library that provides data for the current financial status as well as providing a financial history. The latter is of particular value for establishing parameters for estimating job cost management since it will have detailed job cost figures. **Job cost figures** encompass labor and material costs associated with various facets of design/build or maintenance jobs. These cost figures are vital to the estimating process of landscape contracting. If the business is new, the owner and accountant may utilize industry job cost standards as guidelines (available through trade association publications).

job cost figures
labor and material costs associated with design/build or maintenance jobs.

Since the accuracy of an accounting system depends on the information available, the formatting of accounts should be given careful consideration. Communication between the owner/executive management and the accountant is vital to the immediate and long-term usefulness of the accounting system. As the business expands, the chart of accounts needs to be modified to meet new requirements, for example, the addition of an irrigation division or expanding from design/build to maintenance. The accountant must be made aware of the specific information that management requires. It is then the responsibility of management to meet with project managers and accounting staff to determine what information needs to be categorized into specific accounts. Once the accounts are defined, an integrated accounting system can be developed. It should be a system capable of providing a company with comprehensive financial reports. Each contracting business is unique in terms of its market, services, overhead, and so forth. Therefore, the chart of accounts needs to be customized to meet each company's financial information needs.

ACCOUNT CODING

A coding system enables a company to categorize financial data and to access category summaries individually or in a financial report format. The classification of accounts is standard in all accounting systems. The coding system may be alphabetic or numeric. Some companies prefer the alphabetic coding system because such a system makes it easier to identify accounts than a numeric coding system. In a numeric coding system (Figure 1-7 gives an example), the numbering process begins with a four-digit number that establishes account identification. The first digit represents the account classification, the second two digits are the specific account code number, and the last two digits are a subcode for the respective account. The classification number is specific for each account category, for example, the 1000 series is designated for assets, 2000 for liabili-

```
                    4101
4—account classification, e.g., Income
10—specific account code, e.g., Installation
1—subcode for residential
```

Figure 1-7   Coding System

ties, and so on. When the numeric codes are being assigned, it is important to allow sufficient room between account designations for future expansion.

ACCOUNT CATEGORIES

The chart is comprised of account categories with their respective account listings. Each account category is defined by the individual accounts. The financial data within these accounts provides management with indices for monitoring the account categories. The incorporation of these accounts into financial reports will be discussed and illustrated in Chapter 5, "Financial Management."

balance sheet accounts
all accounts that add financial value to a company and accounts that represent financial obligations of the company.

Balance sheet accounts include all accounts that add financial value to the company and accounts that represent financial obligations of the company. Accounts that comprise a balance sheet include assets and liabilities.

Assets are items that are owned by the company and that have cash value (see Figure 1-8):

> **Current assets**—items that will be transformed into cash within a twelve-month period.

> **Fixed assets**—items that have a long-term value, many of which are depreciated (expensed) over a period of years.

The descending order in which the asset accounts are listed reflects their degree of liquidity (conversion into cash).

liabilities
are all debts incurred by a company.

net worth or **owner's equity**
is the cumulative amount of money that is comprised of accumulated company profits, owner's investment, and owner's after-tax profits.

balance sheet
Reflects the net worth of a company based upon the difference between its total assets and total liabilities.

Liabilities are all debts incurred by a company (see Figure 1-9):

> **Current**—debts that will be paid within a twelve-month period, e.g., vendor invoices, subcontractors.

> **Long-term**—debts that will be paid beyond a twelve-month period, e.g., loans maturing beyond a year, multi-year equipment leases.

Net worth or **owner's equity** is the cumulative amount of money that is comprised of accumulated company profits, owner's investment, and owner's after-tax profits (see Figure 1-10).

The financial data compiled in the balance sheet of accounts enables a balance sheet to be generated. A **balance sheet** reflects the net worth of a company based upon the

Account Number	Account Name	Account Description
	Current Assets	
1001	Cash on premises	Cash funds
1005	Checking accounts	Cumulative cash holdings
1006	Savings accounts	Cumulative cash, e.g., payroll, tax accounts
1011	Investments	Stocks, bonds, certificates of deposit
1030	Accounts receivable—clients	Unpaid invoices, job completions, material sales
1100	Accounts receivable—retainage	Amount of money retained by client, pending job completion
1130	Cost in excess of billing	Value of completed work remaining to be billed
1160	Inventory	Total value of all purchased materials not allocated to jobs
1170	Prepaid expenses	Cumulative payments made prior to due dates, e.g., taxes, insurance, rent
1180	Deposits	Utilities, equipment, rent, etc.
	Fixed Assets	
1190	Land	Original purchase price
1200	Buildings	Original purchase price
1210	Furniture and fixtures	Furniture, fixtures, office equipment, based on purchase price
1220	Construction equipment	Purchase price for all equipment
1250	Maintenance equipment	Purchase price for all equipment
1260	Trucks, trailers, automobiles	Purchase price of all vehicles
1300	Improvements	All permanent improvements made to the company's physical facilities
1350	Depreciation—buildings	Depreciation allowance for account 1200
1400	Depreciation—furniture and fixtures	Depreciation allowance for account 1210
1450	Depreciation—construction equipment	Depreciation allowance for account 1220
1500	Depreciation—maintenance equipment	Depreciation allowance for account 1250
1600	Depreciation—trucks, trailers, automobiles	Depreciation allowance for account 1260
1700	Depreciation—improvements	Depreciation allowance for account 1350

Figure 1-8   1000 Asset Accounts

Account Number	Account Name	Account Description
	Current Liabilities	
2001	Accounts payable— trade	Unpaid invoices from vendors and subcontractors
2030	Accounts payable— retainage	Payments withheld as retainage for subcontractors
2100	Income tax withheld— federal	Federal payroll taxes
2120	Income tax withheld— state	State payroll taxes
2140	FICA tax withheld	Social Security taxes
2160	Notes payable— demand	Loans payable on a date set by the lender, generally short term
2180	Notes payable— current	Loan payments made on a monthly basis, e.g., vehicles, equipment
2200	Capital leases— current	Lease payments made on a monthly basis, e.g., equipment, vehicles
2220	Accrued payroll	Earned wages and salaries remaining to be paid
2230	Accrued insurance	Insurance premiums remaining to be paid
2240	Accrued benefit plan	Payments due the company's compensation plan, e.g., profit sharing, pension fund
2260	Accrued taxes— payroll	Total amount of payroll taxes remaining to be paid
2280	Accrued expenses	Additional expenses, e.g., rent, sales tax, interest
2310	Warranty reserve	Money withheld from sales for warranty replacements
2230	Accrued taxes— income	Amount due to government agencies for taxes on profits
	Long-Term Liabilities	
2500	Notes payable	Bank loans
2550	Notes payable	Equipment
2660	Notes payable	Mortgages with due dates beyond one year

Figure 1-9   2000 Liability Accounts

income statement accounts
reflect all income sources and direct costs associated with generating revenue from profit centers.

direct costs
are costs associated with jobs, such as labor and materials.

profit centers
represent production divisions in a landscape company.

difference between its total assets and total liabilities. This financial report is an indicator of a company's financial stability since it shows whether there are sufficient assets to meet the company's financial obligations (liabilities). The format for a balance sheet is illustrated in Figure 1-11. The financial significance of the balance sheet will be discussed in further detail in Chapter 5.

Income statement accounts include all the accounts that reflect sources of revenue and **direct costs** associated with generating income from profit centers. **Profit centers** represent production divisions in a landscape company.

Account Number	Account Name	Account Description
3001	Common stock	The original issuance value of all shareholder stock
3010	Retained earnings	The accumulated amount of capital from after-tax profits since the company's inception
3020	Net profit—current period	After-tax profits from the current year
3030	Dividends	The distribution of after-tax profits to shareholders

Figure 1-10   3000 Net Worth

Assets
Cash
Cash in accounts
Securities
Accounts receivable—client
Accounts receivable—retainage
Inventory
Other current assets
Fixed assets
    Total current assets

Liabilities & Net Worth
Accounts payable
Notes payable
Other current liabilities
    Total current liabilities
Long-term liabilities
Net worth
    Total liabilities & net worth

Figure 1-11   Balance Sheet

A landscape company generally has different production divisions that contract specific services. These divisions are commonly referred to as profit centers. These centers may provide installation, enhancement, construction, irrigation, commercial maintenance, residential maintenance, snow removal, holiday lighting, pest management, pressure washing, and so forth. It is important to chart separate accounts for these profit centers to enable management to analyze their respective profitability. Each profit center will have either a letter or a numerical code to enable generation of profit and loss statements (income statements; see Figure 1-12).

direct job costs
are all the expenses directly associated with specific contracts, such as labor, materials, and equipment in the company's profit centers.

Direct job costs (Figure 1-13) are all the expenses directly associated with specific contracts, such as labor, materials, and equipment in the company's profit centers. These costs are applied directly to each job in each profit center.

Account Number	Account Name	Account Description
4101	Installation—residential	Revenue from residential design/build installation contracts
4102	Installation—commercial	Commercial design/build installation revenue
4103	Installation—government	Design/build installation revenue from all government contracts
4201	Maintenance—residential	Revenue from residential maintenance contracts
4202	Maintenance—commercial	Revenue from commercial maintenance contracts
4203	Maintenance—government	Revenue from government maintenance contracts
4302	Snow removal—commercial	Revenue from government snow removal contracts
4402	Holiday lighting—commercial	Revenue from holiday light installations
4800	Other income	Interest, investments, rental

Figure 1-12   4000 Income

Account Number	Account Name	Account Description
5100	Plant materials	Subcategories include shrubs, trees, perennials, sod, seasonal color
5200	Hardscape materials	Subcategories include lumber, boulders, gravel, stepping-stones
5300	Freight	Charges associated with plant or hardscape material shipments
5400	Sales tax	All taxes on materials used or sold
5500	Bonds, permits	Costs assigned to respective jobs
5600	Labor	All labor used on the job, inclusive of crew and supervisory personnel
5620	Labor burden	Taxes and benefits for all labor associated with the job
5630	Temporary labor	Labor costs for short-term employees hired for specific jobs
5700	Equipment	Costs assigned to jobs based on time allocated for equipment usage
5800	Equipment rental	Charges assessed to respective jobs
5900	Subcontractors	Expenses associated with all subcontractors contracted on a job

Figure 1-13   5000 Direct Job Cost Accounts

G&A overhead costs

fixed costs that support the sales of goods and services.

fixed costs

are synonomous with general and administrative costs and represent those costs that remain constant regardless of the sales volume. Examples of fixed costs are rent, utilities, advertising, and office expenses.

indirect costs

costs associated with jobs but not involved in the production aspects of jobs.

General and administrative (G&A) overhead costs (Figure 1-14) are categorized into accounts that are inclusive of all costs associated with supporting the sales of goods and services. These costs are generally referred to as **fixed costs** since they remain relatively the same during changes in sales volume. Included in this category of accounts are those referred to as **indirect costs,** costs associated with jobs but not involved in the production aspect of jobs, such as uniforms or small tools.

An illustration of how direct costs may be accessed for a maintenance division analysis is shown in Figure 1-15. The code indicates directs costs designated by 5, with the second digit for the respective cost accounts within this category. The profit center of maintenance is designated by the 2 in the code. These accounts would be broken down further for analysis with subcodes designating residential, commercial, and government contracts. Companies with multiple branches also assign an alphabetical or numerical subcode for the respective branch, for example, B or 3 for Baltimore, A or 5 for Alexandria, and so on.

5102-0203

Direct cost, plant materials, maintenance, commercial, Baltimore branch

income statement

summarizes current revenue, direct and indirect costs, and overhead.

An income statement format that incorporates the financial data contained with the income statement accounts is illustrated in Figure 1-16. The **income statement** is also referred to as a profit and loss statement since it summarizes current revenue, direct and indirect costs, and overhead. This financial report can be generated on a corporate level, for the production division (profit center), or for an individual job.

The chart of accounts presented in this chapter represents the accounting infrastructure that is necessary to build a database for financial management. The number of accounts will vary depending on the amount of financial information that management decides it needs to access. One company may account for plant materials under one account, while another may have subcategories for trees, shrubs, groundcovers, and so on. Its maintenance division may have one account for materials while another company may want to access information on specific materials, such as fertilizers and pesticides. Subsequent chapters will illustrate how the data in the chart of accounts is applied to budget development and financial analyses.

■ Summary

Accounting is a process that records all financial transactions associated with a business. The recorded financial data is classified into income or expenses and posted into account ledgers. The posted data enables management to access the current financial status of individual accounts. The recording and posting of financial data provides the database for generating financial reports. Management's analysis of these reports enables it to determine the current financial status of a company and to render decisions, which will enhance its profitability.

Account Number	Account Name	Account Description
6001	Uniforms	Rental costs prorated over duration of job
6010	Replacement materials	Costs associated with materials and labor for warranty items
6020	Inventory variance	Accounts for inventory losses due to plant death, breakage, and theft
6030	Small tools	Costs associated with small tools used on jobs
6040	Equipment, vehicle maintenance	All costs associated with vehicle and equipment maintenance
6050	Fuel and oil	Equipment and vehicle costs
6070	Insurance—equipment, vehicles	Annual premium costs
6080	Depreciation	Cumulative expense allowance for all owned equipment and vehicles
6090	Leases	Leasing expenses for leased equipment and vehicles
6120	Payroll—mechanics	Salary and benefits
6130	Licenses and fees	Licenses and permit fees for vehicles, trailers
6150	Shop tools, equipment, supplies	Costs associated with shop operation and maintenance
6180	Shop parts inventory	Parts used for equipment and vehicle maintenance
6200	Officer salaries and benefits	Company/corporate officers
6210	Manager salaries	All salaried managers
6220	Clerical salaries and benefits	Administrative staff
6250	Bonuses	Salary incentives/merit increases
6260	Professional services	Legal counsel, payroll processing, accounting, consultation
6280	Utilities	Office, cell phones, radio systems
6370	Maintenance—exterior	All buildings and grounds
6400	Maintenance—office	Office equipment including maintenance contracts
6420	Professional development	Training seminars, conferences, class registration fees, training tapes
6450	Memberships, subscriptions	Professional association dues and publications
6470	Property insurance	All facilities, equipment, liability, theft
6490	Vehicle insurance	All company road-operated vehicles
6500	Marketing	Advertising, promotional items
6520	Donations	Financial and material contributions

Figure 1-14 6000 General and Administrative Overhead Costs

Figure 1-15

Maintenance Cost
Accounts

Account Number	Account Description
5102	Plant materials
5602	Labor
5622	Labor burden
5702	Equipment
5902	Subcontractors
5903	Fertilizers/chemicals

Figure 1-16

Income Statement

Earned Revenue
Net earned revenue

Direct Job Costs
Direct labor
Direct labor burden
Plant materials
Hardscape materials
Material taxes
Subcontractors
Equipment
Other direct job costs
    Total Direct Job Costs

Gross Margin

Indirect Overhead
Indirect labor
Replacement expenses
Small tools and supplies
Equipment rental
Fuel and oil
Other indirect costs
    Total Indirect Overhead

General & Administrative Overhead
Advertising
Depreciation
Insurance—health
Insurance—vehicles

Insurance—liability
Insurance—worker's compensation
Office expense
Utilities
Salaries—officers/owners
Salaries—clerical and administrative
Salaries—sales & commissions
Travel & entertainment
Recruitment
Payroll taxes
Other G&A overhead
    Total General and Administrative Overhead

Operating Profit
Other income—interest
Other expenses
    Net profit before taxes

What are the primary distinctions between accounting methods?

The cash basis of accounting is similar to a checking account with respect to the recording of transactions. This method only records income upon receipt of payments and expenses only as invoices are paid. Therefore the cash basis of accounting does not reflect the actual profitability of a job since the incomes and expenses are distorted. This system does not provide management a resource for making financial decisions.

The accrual basis of accounting is a cumulative system, which records income and expenses as client invoices are issued and vendor invoices are received. The two variations of the accrual method are the billings basis and percentage of completion. The billings basis provides an accurate depiction of income and expenses for short-term jobs in which the client invoices and vendor invoices are recorded within the same period. A more accurate method for reflecting the financial status of an installation job is with the percentage of completion basis of accounting. As each phase of the job is invoiced, all expenses are accounted for on a percentage basis, resulting in 100% accounting for all income and expenses upon job completion. The billings basis accounting method works well with landscape maintenance contracts because total annual costs are prorated over a twelve-month period and billed accordingly. Since the costs are predetermined, an accurate depiction of the contracts financial status is achieved by comparing actual monthly posted costs to the budgeted costs.

What is the function of a chart of accounts?

A chart of accounts is analogous to a business library system. Within the system is financial information, which pertains to every aspect of the business's operations. Management establishes accounts in collaboration with the accountant to provide a database from which financial reports may be derived. In addition, the chart of accounts is vital as a financial history for estimating jobs and monitoring production efficiency. This database of financial information provides a comprehensive profile of the company's net worth and profitability with its integration into balance sheets and income statements.

■■ Knowledge Application

1. Choose a retail garden center in your area. After surveying the facilities and inventory, establish a chart of accounts for income and for direct costs.

2. Using your checkbook, set up a personal ledger sheet with columns for each expense category: for example, books, entertainment, gas, insurance, and so forth. Enter totals for an academic year. Total the columns and calculate the percentage of your total expenses each category represents.

3. Review the liability accounts in the balance sheet of accounts. Select four of these accounts and explain how they might have a negative impact on the financial stability of a company.

CHAPTER 2

Budget Development

CHAPTER OBJECTIVES

To gain an understanding of:

1. The budget development process

2. Budgets as financial tools

3. Profit and why it is the starting point for budget development

4. Budget management as an essential element in financial stability

5. Management reports and interpreting budget variances

KEY TERMS

account managers
add-ons
budget
capital
capital budgets
capital requirement
cash flow budgets
cost structure
depreciation
forecasting
gross margin
net profit
operating budget
principal
profit
profit centers
strategic plans
watchdogs
working capital
zero-based budgeting

budget

projects what revenue will be generated and what expenses will be incurred over a specific period of time.

A budget is a financial game plan for the future. On a personal basis, a **budget** projects what revenue will be generated and what expenses will be incurred over a specific period of time. In the business world, this is referred to as an **operating budget.** It represents an educated guess based on historical financial information. On an individual basis, it would include salary income and expenses, including housing, entertainment, food, automobile expenses, and so on. These projections can then be incorporated into a spreadsheet, which at a glance will reflect positive (revenues exceeds expenses) or negative (expenses exceed revenue) cash flow on a monthly basis. The budget projections enable an individual to anticipate when adjustments need to be made to ensure that there will be sufficient funds to meet projected expenses. These adjustments may require transferring funds from savings, obtaining a loan, or deferring certain purchases. It is therefore evident that a budget is an important financial management tool as well as being a financial barometer.

March Budget

Installation Division	February 28 Budget Actual	March 7 Budget Actual	March 14 Budget Actual	March 21 Budget Actual	March 31 Budget Actual
Revenue					
Total					
Expenses					
Direct costs					
Indirect costs					
Total					
Revenue					
Expenses					
Net profit					

Example of a Budget Spreadsheet for BradCo Landscape Company

operating budget
projects what revenues will be generated and what expenses will be incurred over a specific period of time.

profit
the amount of money left after a company has met its current financial obligations.

In the business environment, budget development is vital to a company's financial health, growth, and development. If it is managed astutely, the company will be profitable, enabling it to reinvest its profits for future growth, retire debt, provide additional compensation for employees, and fulfill its tax liabilities (Figure 2-1). **Profit** is the amount of money that is left after a company has met all of its current financial obligations.

An operating budget relies on financial data from previous years for its projections of revenues and expenses. Since a budget is considered a best educated guess, it serves as a financial blueprint for building a structure for financial management. The budget is revisited on a regular basis, such as quarterly, and adjustments are made for variables such as weather, the economy, and new sales opportunities.

Most importantly, a company's operating budget is its daily financial report card. It enables management to communicate the current financial status of the company, branch, or division to the respective managers. Managers can compare actual financial figures against the budgeted amounts and determine where adjustments need to be made to stay

- Debt payments—bank loans, etc.
- Equipment purchases
- Working capital—cash for projected growth
- Bonuses, profit sharing, pension contributions, tax liabilities—city, county, state, federal

Figure 2-1 Profit Allocation

on target for the company's projected profit. The budget is the most important tool in the financial toolbox. It is a tool that enables managers to be proactive in monitoring and making adjustments in labor and material costs to ensure profitability.

Other budgets utilized by companies include:

cash flow budgets
project cash balances over a specific period of time: monthly, quarterly, or annually.

- **Cash flow budgets,** which project cash balances over a specific period of time: monthly, quarterly, or annually. These budgets alert management to the need to secure loans or to apply cash reserves during periods when there are cash shortages (due to expenses exceeding revenue).

capital budgets
are developed to allocate money for purchases of assets such as vehicles and equipment.

- **Capital budgets,** which are developed to allocate money for purchases of assets such as vehicles and equipment.

The discussion in this chapter is directed toward operating budgets since they are a company's primary financial management tool.

The operating budget development process is illustrated in Figure 2-2. As illustrated, the budget is profit driven. Key components of this process are costs, direct, indirect, and overhead, derived from the chart of accounts. These costs provide parameters for establishing budgets. They are calculated as a percentage of sales. When sales are projected for subsequent years, the cost parameters are applied to establish corresponding costs. Additional components include revenue/sales projections and the **capital,** which is the money needed to support the increased sales. The forecasting discussion that follows explains how capital requirements are determined for projected increases in revenues. The support relates primarily to additional personnel and equipment.

capital
the money needed to support increased sales.

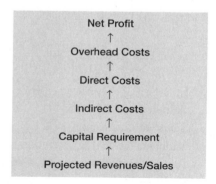

Net Profit
↑
Overhead Costs
↑
Direct Costs
↑
Indirect Costs
↑
Capital Requirement
↑
Projected Revenues/Sales

Figure 2-2 Operating Budget Development

Each of the budget development components is critical to the end product, which serves as a comprehensive financial plan for the future. The budget serves as a barometer, enabling management to track whether the company is on target to meet its projected profit.

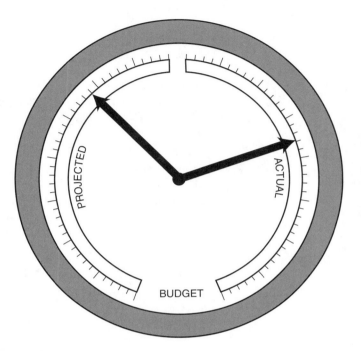

Budget Barometer

■ Forecasting

forecasting

a process that determines the working capital, asset, and personnel needs for projected revenues.

Forecasting is a process that determines the working capital, asset, and personnel needs for projected revenues. These determinations are based on financial data in the company's database. In the example that follows, a forecast is developed for the BradCo Landscape Company, an exterior maintenance company. Its financial data includes the following:

Costs based on percent of sales:	Direct—54%
	Indirect—10%
	Overhead—30%
Financial ratios:	Sales/total assets—3.5
	Sales/working capital—12
Marketing ratios:	Maintenance contract retention—90%
	Additional maintenance sales—$.25 per dollar of contracted sales
	New sales per salesperson—$300,000

Company ratios: Sales per full-time employee (FTE)—$55,000

Employee turnover—30%

Business per account manager—$750,000

Business per maintenance crew—$250,000

Administrative staff to $1 million in sales—l:1

FORECASTING

Revenue	Labor	Administrative Personnel	Capital Assets	Fixed Assets

BradCo Landscape Company Forecast

The cost percentages were derived from last year's income statement (Figure 2-3). They represent their respective percentage of the total company's sales; for example, 54% direct costs ($1,458,000/$2,750,000). Before these cost parameters are utilized in the forecasting process, the percentages need to be validated as being representative of previous years. New businesses can obtain guidelines for the above benchmarks by referring to the *Operating Cost Study* compiled by PLANET (Professional Landcare Network) and ANLA (American Nursery & Landscape Association). This study profiles landscape contracting businesses within specific sales volumes and their respective costs of operation. The figures that will be used in the subsequent company example are within the range of those noted in the industry survey.

net profit

the amount of money that remains after costs (direct, indirect, and overhead) have been paid and before taxes are paid.

The management of the BradCo Landscape Company has determined that it can increase next year's sales by 20% and improve bottom line net profit from 6% to 10%. **Net profit** is the amount of money that remains from revenues when all costs (direct, indirect, and overhead) have been paid and before taxes are paid.

2004 Income Statement

Net Sales	**$2,750,000**	**100%**
Direct Job Costs		
Direct labor	825,000	30.0
Direct labor burden	82,500	3.0
Material costs	440,000	16.0
Subcontractors	110,000	4.0
Other	27,500	1.0
Total Direct Job Costs	**$1,485,000**	**54%**
Gross Profit Margin	**$1,265,000**	**46%**
Indirect Costs		
Indirect labor	96,250	3.5
Replacement expenses	8,250	.3
Small tools & supplies	27,500	1.0
Equipment rental	33,000	1.2
Fuel & oil	55,000	2.0
Other	55,000	2.0
Total Indirect Job Costs	**$275,000**	**10%**
General & Administrative Overhead		
Advertising	27,500	1.0
Depreciation	82,500	3.0
Insurance—hospital	41,250	1.5
Insurance—liability	27,500	1.0
Insurance—workers compensation	41,250	1.5
Office expense	27,500	1.0
Payroll taxes	27,500	1.0
Profit sharing	13,750	.5
Lease/land, facilities	82,500	3.0
Salaries—owners	192,500	7.0
Salaries—administrative	137,500	5.0
Salaries—sales	8,250	.3
Telephone/radios/office equipment	33,000	1.2
Utilities	8,250	.3
Other	74,250	2.7
Total G&A Overhead	**$825,000**	**30%**
Net Pretax Profit	**$165,000**	**6%**

Figure 2-3   BradCo Landscape Company 2004 Income Statement

To meet the revenue and profit goals, capital, personnel, sales, and asset requirements must be determined. The five-step forecasting process, proposed by Kevin Kehoe, business consultant, illustrates how these determinations are calculated:

I. Sales and Net Profit Determination

	Current	Next Year	Increase
Sales	$2,750,000	$3,300,000	20%
Net profit	165,000	330,000	4%

A projected sales increase of 20% over last year's sales is $3,300,000 ($2,750,000 + $550,00). The projected net profit of 10% for next year's sales of $3,300,000 is $330,000.

II. Determination of Capital Requirement

	Current	Next Year	Increase
Sales	$2,750,000	$3,300,000	$550,000
Working capital	229,167	275,000	45,833
Fixed assets	556,547	667,857	113,310
Total assets	785,714	942,857	158,143

working capital
the amount of money needed to support projected growth (increased revenues).

Using the current year's sales and working capital figures, $2,750,000/229,167, a sales/working capital ratio of 12:1 is established. **Working capital** is the amount of money (cash) that is required to support projected growth (increased revenues). This ratio indicates that an additional $1 is needed for every $12 increase in sales. Applying this ratio to next year's sales increase of $550,000 indicates that an additional $45,833 ($550,000/12) of capital will be required to support next year's sales. The total capital requirement for next year of $275,000 is determined by adding the $45,833 to the current year's working capital requirement of $229,167. The sales/assets ratio of 3.50 ($2,750,000/$785,714) represents an additional $1 of assets required for every $3.50 increase in sales. Based upon next year's projected sales increase, an additional amount of $157,143 ($550,000/3.5) is needed in total assets. The total asset requirement of $942,857 for the next year is determined by adding the $157,143 to the current year's assets of $785,714. The total assets figure reflects what is available for equipment purchases (as well as other fixed assets) and working capital (cash). The required fixed assets amount, $667,857, is determined by subtracting the working capital, $275,000, from the total assets, $942,857.

add-ons
additional sales beyond the current contract.

Once the sales volume has been projected, the next step in the forecasting process is determining what the sales requirement (Step III) will be to meet the 20% increase. The starting point for this determination is the maintenance company's contract retention rate. Last year's total sales of $2,750,000 had base sales of $2,062,500 ($2,750,000 − $687,500 add-ons). **Add-ons** represent additional sales beyond the current contract, such as for landscape renovations or seasonal color. The $687,500 represents add-on sales of $.25 per dollar of contract. Based upon a 90% contract retention (based on contract renewals) the BradCo Landscape Company's next year's base sales are projected at $1,856,250 (90% of $2,062,500). In order to attain the company's sales goal of $3,300,000 an additional $1,443,750 ($3,300,000 − $1,856,250) in sales will have to be obtained. Of the $1,443,750 sales balance, add-on sales will amount to $464,062 ($.25 × $1,856,250), leaving $979,688 ($1,443,750 − $464,062) to be obtained through new maintenance contract sales.

III. Determination of New Sales Requirement

	Current	Next Year
Base sales	$2,062,500	$1,856,250
Add-ons	687,500	464,062
New contract sales		979,688
Total sales	$2,750,000	$3,300,000

One of the greatest challenges facing the landscape industry is maintaining a sufficient labor force to meet its current and future needs. When sales projections are made, this challenge is further accentuated. The fourth step in the forecasting process determines personnel requirements for the projected revenues.

profit centers
revenue-generating divisions.

Determination of production personnel requirements starts with totaling the production hours for all profit centers. **Profit centers** are revenue-generating divisions, e.g., maintenance, installation, irrigation, etc. Only the hours of FTEs (full-time employees) are included in the total. FTEs are production personnel who have worked 2,100 hours per year (the total varies by region). Of the 2,100 hours, 1,800 have been documented, in our example, to be production related. The total current year's production hours for the BradCo Landscape Company are 108,000 (1,800 × 60 FTEs). The sales per FTE were calculated to be $46,000 ($2,750,000/108,000 hrs × 1,800 hrs). Applying this sales/FTE to next year's forecast determines that 72 FTEs ($3,300,000/$46,000) are required to generate $3,300,000 in total production sales.

Next year's sales require 12 more FTEs than the previous year. In addition to recruiting 12 production personnel, the BradCo Landscape Company needs to hire an additional 18 employees to account for employee turnover (.30 × 60). Therefore, the total number of FTE production personnel to be recruited for next year is 30 (18 + 12).

Administrative support is critical to the support of increased sales, particularly from the perspective of contract management and accounting. Industry surveys indicate that one administrative staff employee is required for every million dollars in revenues. Based upon next year's projected revenues, 3.3 employees are required for administrative staff, or three full-time employees and one part-time employee.

account managers
those who manage company contracts.

Another key personnel area that needs to be addressed is account managers. **Account managers** (of maintenance companies) are individuals who manage company contracts. The amount of revenue that an account manager is capable of managing effectively, particularly regarding maintaining client relations and production standards, depends on several variables. These include the size and services of the maintenance sites, supervisor proficiency levels, and distances between client properties. The company in our example has assessed the amount of revenue per account manager to be

$800,000. On this basis, its next year's increased revenue projection of $550,000 does not warrant hiring an additional account manager, but it may justify grooming an individual in an assistant account manager position for future promotion.

IV. Determination of Personnel Requirements

	Current	Next Year
Sales	$2,750,000	$3,300,000
Sales per employee	46,000	46,000
Number FTEs	60	72
Turnover rate	30%	
Recruiting needs	20	30
Administrative needs	2.75	3.3
Additional account managers		1

The final step in the planning process establishes the budget parameters for all the expenses associated with the company's projected revenues. The company's financial ratios (costs/sales) are used to establish these financial parameters.

V. Budget Parameters

Sales	$3,300,000	100%
Direct costs	1,782,000	54%
Indirect costs	330,000	10%
Overhead costs	858,000	26%
Net Profit	330,000	10%

The financial information detailed above now enables the BradCo Landscape Company to develop an operating budget that incorporates the expenses associated with the projected growth. The company's capital budget will incorporate the amount of money required for purchase of assets (e.g., equipment) to support next year's revenue projections. Management's budget discussions will therefore be based upon realistic expectations rather than suppositions based upon anticipated needs.

■ Budget Development Process

The preceding forecasting process initiated the framing of the operating budget. The remaining infrastructure is built upon the best educated guess scenario within divisions and branches regarding their respective budgets. The finalized company budget expresses in dollars, on a month-to-month basis, the progression of revenues and expenses for the entire company. As previously stated, budgets are profit driven, and therefore, cost accountability is critical to ensure attaining the company's profit goal. The financial data in the chart of accounts collectively become the building blocks for constructing a budget.

Simplification of the budgeting process can be detrimental to a company because of the inaccuracies that then become manifested in the final budget. Budgeting methods that are indicative of such inaccuracies include the following:

Growth rate method—Projects revenue increase based on last year's growth. It makes the erroneous assumption that variables will remain constant. Personnel and equipment needs are not taken into account to meet the revenue goal.

Percentage method—A method that selects a desired percentage of revenue increase and uses it as a parameter for estimating costs. The fallacy of this method is that it assumes costs will increase proportionally to the percentage of increased revenues.

Inflation rate—This method reflects back on last year's inflation rate and adjusts budgeted expenses by the respective rate. As with the percentage method, costs cannot be equated to an external factor.

A misconception among those who use the growth rate and percentage basis methodology is that revenues are the primary entity that drives the budgeting process. Have you ever heard a person say that he or she is in business to generate revenues? Or that an investor selects a company's stock solely on its revenues? The answer is an emphatic no. Profit is what businesses strive for and depend upon for their growth. A key point to remember is that increased revenues do not necessarily generate increased profit.

Profit therefore becomes the starting point for the budgeting process. The BradCo Landscape Company management determines how much profit is needed based upon the items in Figure 2-4.

principal
the total dollar amount of a
loan without interest.

The profit requirement determination begins with the principal associated with debt that must be paid within the year. The **principal** is the total dollar amount of a loan without interest. The interest is not included in this calculation, since it is budgeted over the twelve months as an overhead expense. Principal associated with debt is separated into that which is associated with bank loans, $62,600 in this case, and that of fixed asset acquisitions, $113,310.

B C L C	
• Principal payments on debt	$ 62,600
• Fixed asset acquisitions	113,310
• Cash/working capital required	55,000
• Estimated excess compensation	58,000
• Income tax liability	66,000
• Total Capital Requirement	$354,910
• Estimated depreciation	(113,964)
• Profit Requirement	$240,946

Figure 2-4   Profit Requirement Determination

When reference is made to fixed assets, the asset in question is primarily equipment. The revenue projection stipulated in the previous company example was $3,300,000, which represented a $550,000 increase in revenues. Budgeting the **capital requirement** to support the growth entails dividing the dollar increase by a factor of 10. The factor derivation comes from the banking industry, which has established that 10 cents is needed to support every $1 of earned revenues in the Green Industry. The sales growth projection therefore has a capital requirement of $55,000 (adjusted from the forecasted $45,833). Design/build companies that maintain large material inventories would apply the 15/$1 of earned revenues.

An additional profit need determination of $28,000 must be made for excess compensation, bonuses, profit sharing, or pension plans, since there isn't another source to fund this expense.

Allocation of profit for tax liabilities is another determination entity, one that will vary from state to state. In the example, an estimate (20%) of state, county, and federal taxes on projected profit amounts to a tax liability of $66,000.

The total capital requirement for the BradCo Landscape Company to meet its financial liabilities, support growth, and provide for excess compensation is $284,910. Deducted from this amount is depreciation of $113,964. **Depreciation** is a tax allowance for the decreased value of equipment and vehicles. The balance of $170,946 is the minimum amount of profit needed to meet the company's financial liabilities.

Budgeting general and administrative overhead expenses is the next step in the process. The accounts associated with this category of expenses are listed in the company's profit and loss statement (Figure 2-3). They comprise all of the expenses associated with the cost of doing business: administrative salaries, professional development, equipment maintenance, and so forth. Management assesses each of these accounts on the dollar amount needed to support projected revenues. Therefore, last year's figures or percentages are not automatically inserted into the next year's budget. Instead, it is advisable for companies to use zero-based budgeting. **Zero-based budgeting** projects account costs based on future needs rather than on historical data. On this basis, each expense must be justified in regard to how it helps to achieve the company's financial goals. In the budgeting discussions, managers may, for example, decide that the $50,000 equipment parts inventory can be reduced, since parts are readily available from local sources. Since these overhead costs account for approximately 25%, management tries to reduce expenses wherever feasible.

Further consideration is also given to strategic plan goals that are to be implemented in the coming year. **Strategic plans** specify goals and strategies to achieve them within a specific period of time, generally three to five years. One of these goals may be to increase residential design/build sales through participation in a local garden show. The cost of this involvement would be added to the advertising budget.

The overhead expense sheet in Figure 2-5 is a useful tool for analyzing accounts as to how well they support next year's projected revenues. Prior to budgeting the account expense, management does an analysis of the company's advertising program and its current return (sales generated) on invested dollars. Since referrals are a primary

capital requirement
10 to 15 cents on each dollar of increased revenues.

depreciation
a tax allowance for the decreased value of equipment and vehicles.

zero-based budgeting
projects account costs based on future needs rather than historical data.

strategic plans
specify goals and strategies to achieve them within a specific period of time.

BradCo Landscape Company

Division: Residential Installation

Budget Year: 2004

Account Number: 7000

Account title: Advertising

Description: All expenses associated with enhancing the sales of residential installation such as brochures, ads, and garden show displays are included in this account.

Cost Projections:

Expense	Quantity	Unit Cost	Total Cost
Ads—Maryland Living	4	$ 1,200	$ 4,800
Garden show displays	1	30,000	30,000
Miscellaneous ads	4	250	1,000
Total: Last year $28,200			$35,800

Monthly Advertising Allocation:

Jan.	$1,200	Feb.	$30,000	March	$1,200	April	$1,450
May	$250	June	$250	July	0	August	0
Sept.	$250	Oct.	$1,200	Nov.	0	Dec.	0

Figure 2-5   Overhead Expense Sheet

source of new business for landscape companies, all advertising dollars need to be justified on the basis of tracking new business associated with the respective advertising venues. Management decided, on the basis of their anlaysis, that the *Maryland Living* magazine ads provided name recognition but did not warrant more than four ads. In addition, after two years of tracking referrals from participation in showcase home exhibits, it was decided that the associated expense was not warranted. A decision was made to reallocate the showcase home dollars to the local garden show. Feedback from industry colleagues regarding job referrals and attendance influenced this decision.

watchdogs

monitor specific overhead accounts throughout the budget year.

Management often will assign **watchdogs** to monitor specific overhead accounts throughout the budget year (Figure 2-6). The assigned managers ensure that the budgeted expense for their respective accounts does not deviate from its projection.

A twelve-month spreadsheet of the budgeted overhead expenses enables close monitoring with the actual expenses incurred. On a month-to-month basis, any indication of deviations from the budgeted expenses will enable management to determine where adjustments need to be made to stay on target to meet the budgeted figures.

Overhead Account Management Record

Division: Maintenance

Budget Year: 2004

Watchdog: Todd

Account Number: 6030

Account Title: Small tools

Annual Projections:

Item	Qty.	Unit Cost	Total Cost
Grass rakes	30	$15	$ 450
Long handled shovels	20	18	360
Trowels	50	5	250
Steel tine rakes	20	18	360
Gloves	60	8	480
2003 Total $1,765			$1,900

Figure 2-6   Watchdog Account Management

The next step in finalizing an operating budget is to combine the total annual expenses (Figure 2-7). In essence, management generates a projected income statement, itemizing expenses as a percentage of projected revenue. In some cases, financial history is utilized if the expenses as a percentage of sales have been consistent. The balance of expenses is projected based on management's assessment of need (zero-based budgeting). This financial data is then distributed over a twelve-month period based on trends established from historical data (monthly revenue and expenses). The finalized monthly income statement becomes a working document, which is revisited on a daily basis. If there appears to be a major deviation from projections, for example, due to weather, unanticipated new sales, or cancelled contracts, the budget will be adjusted, generally on a quarterly basis. The importance of monitoring the budget on a daily basis is emphasized by the following statement,

"Real-time budgeting improves reaction time and enhances profitability."
Charlie Bowers, President, Garden Gate Landscape Company.

2005 Projected Income Statement

Revenues	**$3,300,000**	**100%**
Direct Job Costs		
Direct labor	990,000	30.0
Direct labor burden	99,000	3.0
Material costs	528,000	16.0
Subcontractors	132,000	4.0
Other	33,000	1.0
Total Direct Job Costs	**$1,782,000**	**54%**
Gross Margin	**$1,518,000**	**46%**
Indirect Costs		
Indirect labor	49,500	1.5
Warranty expenses	9,900	.3
Small tools & supplies	33,000	1.0
Equipment rental	39,600	1.2
Fuel & oil	66,000	2.0
Other	66,000	2.0
Total Indirect Job Costs	**$264,000**	**8%**
General & Administrative Overhead		
Advertising	33,000	1.0
Depreciation	99,000	3.0
Insurance—hospital	49,500	1.5
Insurance—liability	33,000	1.0
Insurance—workers compensation	49,500	1.5
Office expense	33,000	1.0
Payroll taxes	33,000	1.0
Profit sharing	16,500	.5
Lease/land, facilities	99,000	3.0
Salaries—owners	231,000	7.0
Salaries—administrative	165,000	5.0
Salaries—sales	9,900	.3
Telephone/radios/office equipment	39,600	1.2
Utilities	9,900	.3
Other	23,100	.7
Total G&A Overhead	**$924,000**	**28%**
Net Pretax Profit	**$330,000**	**10%**

Figure 2-7   BradCo Landscape Company 2005 Projected Income Statement

The monthly distribution of projected expenses and revenue is made on an income statement. Incorporating actual figures adjacent to the budgeted projections provides instant awareness of the current financial status of the company.

The projected income statement (Figure 2-7) establishes a **cost structure** that reflects what percentages of revenues will be accounted for by costs. These percentages be-

cost structure
reflects the percentages of revenues accounted for by costs.

come icons within a budget for managing costs. One of the most critical of the structure components is direct costs. This component will determine whether the projected gross margin percentage is attained. The **gross margin** is the amount of money that is left after direct costs are paid. If the projected gross margin percentage (46%) is not attained due to over-budget direct costs, then the bottom line profit projection (10%) will not be met. Since indirect costs ($264,000) and overhead costs ($924,000) are deducted from the gross margin dollars, a reduced amount directly impacts net profit dollars. To ensure that this gross margin goal is met, management places high priority on the management of the direct costs.

gross margin
the amount of money left after direct costs are paid.

Accounting departments post revenues and expenses as they are incurred and provide spreadsheets of the budget that show actual expenses and revenues adjacent to the projected figures. At a glance, managers can then ask why specific costs are over budget. If the cost is labor, then a weekly job cost analysis will be done to detect where the additional hours have been expended.

The monthly distribution of projected revenues and expenses actually establishes monthly income statements. Based on the seasonal patterns of the landscape industry, monthly figures will reflect a profit or loss. Maintenance companies that prorate annual contracts over a twelve-month period (e.g., $60,000 contract, $5,000/month) find that their costs will exceed revenue during the peak season and therefore show a loss for several months. Since these companies receive the same revenue flow in the off season, November–March, when labor costs (in regard to servicing the contracts) are lower, they will actually show a profit in the off season.

A monthly budget report enables management to immediately see variances (Figure 2-8). The red flags raised by the over-budget direct costs and indirect costs alerts management to production problems with one or more of its profit centers. Once the source(s) of the variances is determined, an analysis of job cost reports will be made. In this example, management may detect an excess of hours expended on one or more maintenance services, such as mulching or pruning associated with specific accounts. Further analysis may indicate that excess travel time due to road construction contributed to the increase in production hours.

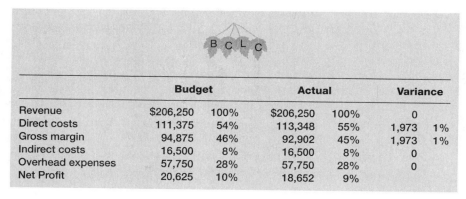

	Budget		Actual		Variance	
Revenue	$206,250	100%	$206,250	100%	0	
Direct costs	111,375	54%	113,348	55%	1,973	1%
Gross margin	94,875	46%	92,902	45%	1,973	1%
Indirect costs	16,500	8%	16,500	8%	0	
Overhead expenses	57,750	28%	57,750	28%	0	
Net Profit	20,625	10%	18,652	9%		

Figure 2-8   BradCo Landscape Company March Budget Report

	Annual	January	February	March	April	May	June
Revenue	**$625,000**	**$11,875**	**$9,375**	**$22,750**	**$47,062**	**$97,185**	**$90,375**
Direct Costs							
Plants	$156,655	$1,550	$1,350	$4,471	13,052	$26,100	$18,228
Hardscape	45,032	967	1,150	2,712	6,059	8,022	8,618
Labor	92,356	2,506	2,337	6,490	10,825	11,350	11,043
Labor B	18,471	512	467	1,181	2,165	22,650	2,210
Subcont.	20,698	0	0	0	2,250	3,125	5,750
Total	332,212	$5,535	$5,304	$14,854	$34,351	$71,247	$45,849
G Margin	**$292,788**	**$6,340**	**$4,071**	**$7,896**	**$12,711**	**$25,938**	**$44,526**
Overhead Costs							
Indirect Costs	**$48,079**	**$4,582**	**$3,562**	**$3,688**	**$5,813**	**$4,850**	**$4,281**
Equipment Costs	**$20,180**	**$1,193**	**$1,225**	**$1,451**	**$2,169**	**$2,225**	**$2,539**
Admin.	**$154,993**	**$13,821**	**$12,912**	**$11,512**	**$14,118**	**$11,962**	**$11,061**
Total OH	**$223,252**	**$19,596**	**$17,699**	**$16,651**	**$22,100**	**$18,797**	**$20,881**
Net Profit	**$69,536**	**($13,256)**	**($13,628)**	**($8,755)**	**($10,611)**	**$7,141**	**$23,375**

Figure 2-9 Monthly Budget Projections for BradCo Landscape Company Installation Division

The company's operating budget is delineated into division budgets as indicated in Figure 2-9. The manager of BradCo's installation division will compare actual cost and revenue figures against the projected budget and be proactive in making the necessary adjustments. The actual budget figures are a direct reflection of the manager's management abilities.

The monthly distribution of projected revenues and expenses, as in Figure 2-9, creates monthly income statements. Based on the seasonal patterns of the landscape industry, monthly figures will reflect a profit or loss. This is illustrated in the six-month budget for BradCo Landscape Company's installation division.

Maintenance companies bill their clients on a monthly basis, prorating the total dollar amount of the contracts over a twelve-month period. In this monthly budget, there are several months in which costs exceed revenue, reflecting losses. This occurs during the peak season when labor hours are high due to the delivered services. Since the revenue is constant over the twelve-month period, profitable months for the maintenance sector are in the off season (November–March), when labor costs (in regard to servicing the contracts) are lower.

Daily and weekly budget reports enable a manager to immediately see where the budget is off track. Then adjustments can be made to offset a decrease in gross margin. There may have been extenuating circumstances, such as equipment breakdowns that resulted in higher labor costs from overtime charges. In this situation, the manager may decide to allocate additional equipment and personnel to complete the job in a shorter period of time, thereby bringing down the unit cost of labor. If the equipment cost is over budget, it may be due to the fact that the equipment is being used for only two hours but is being charged against the job for eight hours. Scheduling the equipment with other managers would result in more efficient use of the equipment and a reduction in overhead.

An operating budget is a financial tool that management must skillfully employ to enhance bottom line profit.

■ Summary

What is the budget development process?

It is a process that projects a company's revenues and expenses over a specific period of time. Operating budgets are developed for the overall company and further delineated into division budgets.

The development process engages management in forecasting revenues, personnel, working capital, and fixed assets; determining profit requirements; establishing a cost structure as a percentage of revenues; and projecting overhead costs.

Why is profit a starting point for budget development?

"Work without profit is exercise; work with profit is business." Profit is the starting point because it is required to retire debt, provide excess compensation for personnel, purchase fixed assets, and provide capital for implementation of strategic plan goals.

How are budgets used as financial tools?

Budgets reflect the current financial status of a company or division in relation to actual expenses and revenues to budgeted projections. Managers use these tools to detect variances and determine factors contributing to the variances.

How does budget management contribute to financial stability?

Budgets are a road map to a company's profitability. Budget management ensures that budget projections are met and that profitability is enhanced. Adjustments are made when necessary to keep the budget on track toward the profit goal.

How are variances in budget reports interpreted?

Managers access daily reports that indicate variances from budget projections. Interpretation involves investigating factors contributing to the respective budget line and determining where adjustments can be made.

■■■ Knowledge Application

1. Develop an annual budget based on your anticipated salary and living expenses. Distribute your expenses (rent, automobile insurance, entertainment, and so forth) and income on a monthly basis based on when they occur.

2. University Landscape Company, with nine FTEs and sales of $500,000, and based on sales of $55,000/employee, projects an increase in sales next year of $200,000. How many FTEs will be required to meet this projection? The company has a 30% employee turnover rate.

3. You are a profit center manager who is in the process of developing your annual budget. The company president has offered managers a bonus incentive of $1,000 for every 1% increase they achieve in their gross margin. How would you manage your budget to be eligible for the bonus incentive?

4. Landscape company A, with gross sales of $700,000, has an annual net profit of 6%, while landscape company B, with the same sales volume, has a net profit of 10%. Illustrate in a budget format the net profits as stated. Explain your cost allocations in regard to their influence on the respective net profits.

Profitable Pricing

CHAPTER OBJECTIVES

To gain an understanding of:

1. Pricing components and their significance to price determination

2. The pricing formula's application to the landscape industry

3. Hourly rate determination for labor and equipment

4. Markup and how it is calculated for labor and materials

5. The dual overhead recovery method, its calculation and application

KEY TERMS

breakeven point

direct costs

dual overhead rate
    method

labor burden

materials to labor ratio

overhead

overhead markup

profit

profit markup

The title of this chapter appears to be stating the obvious. After all, why would any business not price its product profitably? It wouldn't do so intentionally, but if its management lacks an understanding of price components, it can very easily perpetuate unprofitable pricing. These components are **direct costs, overhead,** and **profit,** which collectively contribute to the pricing process.

direct costs, overhead, profit collectively contribute to the pricing process.

The pricing process provides an objective basis, utilizing a company's financial data, for determining a selling price. Without this process, pricing is a shot in the dark, particularly when it entails trying to meet the competition's low price. This is a dangerous road that often leads to a dead end or, in business terms, a bankruptcy. Remember those lumberyards and hardware stores that tried to compete on price with Home Depot? Where are they today? The same place as those electronics stores that tried to compete with Best Buy and Circuit City. But in spite of the presence of food warehouses and Wal-Mart, there are still a plethora of supermarkets. How have they survived? Their survival can be attributed to their management's pricing structure that accounts for costs and profit. That is precisely what this chapter will emphasize: pricing for profit.

Direct Costs	+	Overhead Costs	+	Profit	=	Selling Price
Labor costs		Administrative salaries		Growth capital		
Materials		Travel		Debt retirement		
Equipment		Maintenance shop		Fixed asset purchases		
Subcontracts		Sales department		Bonuses		
		Equipment maintenance		Income tax		
		Advertising				

■ "Work without profit is exercise, work with profit is business." ■

■ Material Markup

Pricing is not as simple as assigning a dollar figure to a product or service. When a retail nursery prices a 2.5" caliper tree, the determination is based on the wholesale cost (direct cost) plus a percentage over that cost to recover overhead expense. This percentage increase is referred to as an **overhead markup.** The overhead markup (OM) is calculated by dividing the overhead expenses by the material costs:

Overhead markup = Overhead expenses / Material costs

Once the nursery adds the overhead markup to the material cost, the price represents a **breakeven point,** having recovered the direct cost of the tree and the overhead expenses associated with its sale.

Using the percentage indicated in the income statement (Figure 3-1), the final calculation involves a **profit markup** on the breakeven price (Figure 3-2).

overhead markup
added to the direct cost to recover overhead expenses.

breakeven point
where the price includes direct costs and overhead costs.

profit markup
added to the breakeven price to calculate the selling price.

Terrapin Nursery

Total revenue	$600,000	100%
Direct costs		
Material	$330,000	55%
Total direct costs	$330,000	55%
Gross margin	$270,000	45%
Overhead costs	$210,000	35%
Net Profit	$ 60,000	10%

Figure 3-1 Terrapin Nursery Income Statement

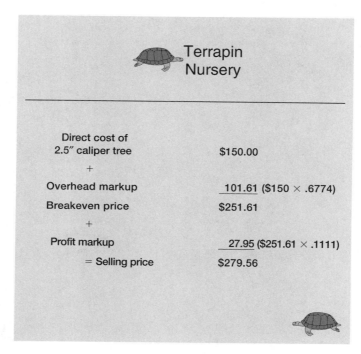

Figure 3-2 Nursery Price Determination

The nursery example illustrates an application of the overhead markup process that is applicable to a typical retail business whose revenue is based solely upon the sale of merchandise or materials. Since all of the overhead expenses (sales personnel, rent, insurance, vehicles, and so forth) of such businesses are associated with supporting the sale of the merchandise, the overhead markup calculation is simple:

$$\$210,000 \text{ (Overhead)}/\$330,000 \text{ (Material costs)} = 67.74\%$$

The profit markup was calculated using the complement of the profit percentage (Figure 3-3). The complement of a profit percentage is determined by dividing the desired profit percentage (10%) by the difference between that percentage and 100% (90%):

$$.10/.90 = .1111$$

The selling price can also be calculated by dividing the breakeven price by the inverse of the desired profit percentage:

$$\$251.61/.90 = \$279.56$$

The inverse figures from Figure 3-3 represent the reciprocal of the desired profit percentage, e.g., .90 is the inverse of a desired 10% net profit.

Desired Percent Net Profit	Inverse Factor: Divide into Breakeven	Complement Factor: Multiply Breakeven
1.00	.99	.0101
2.00	.98	.0204
3.00	.97	.0309
4.00	.96	.0417
5.00	.95	.0526
6.00	.94	.0638
7.00	.93	.0753
8.00	.92	.0870
9.00	.91	.0989
10.00	.90	.1111
11.00	.89	.1236
12.00	.88	.1364
13.00	.87	.1494
14.00	.86	.1628
15.00	.85	.1765
16.00	.84	.1905
17.00	.83	.2048
18.00	.82	.2195
19.00	.81	.2346
20.00	.80	.2500
25.00	.75	.3333
30.00	.70	.4286
40.00	.60	.6666
50.00	.50	1.000

Figure 3-3 Profit Markup Factors

Source: Pricing for the Green Industry, Frank H. Ross, Ross/Payne & Associates, 2nd edition, © 1997, Professional Landcare Network, Herndon, VA.

Why not make life simple and just calculate the profit markup by multiplying the breakeven price by .10? The reason is illustrated by the following example:

Direct cost of 2.5″ caliper tree	$150.00
+	
Overhead markup	101.61 ($150 × .6774)
Breakeven price	$251.61
+	
Profit markup	25.16 ($251.61 × .10)
= Selling Price	$276.77

The profit markup calculated with the desired profit percentage actually represents a 9% ($25.16/$276.77) markup rather than the projected 10%. The $2.79 difference in price is insignificant on an individual tree sale, but it becomes significant when this 9%

markup is applied to the sale of multiple trees. Five hundred 2.5" caliper trees priced with a 9% markup would represent a difference in revenue of $1,395 less than those priced with the complement profit markup based on the desired 10% profit.

It is apparent by the previous pricing example that a profit markup miscalculation of only 1% can have a major negative impact on a company's profitability. The cumulative effect of such a miscalculation results in less profit to reinvest in the company's future growth.

The pricing process becomes more complex for a landscape contracting business whose revenue is generated by the sale of labor, materials, equipment, and subcontracts. In addition, landscape companies have multiple divisions, such as maintenance, installation, enhancement, construction, and irrigation, all of which have their own respective labor and equipment rates. Therefore, when a landscape company prices its jobs, it must have a comprehensive financial database for each division. Updates to the database are imperative to account for increases in direct and overhead costs, such as material costs, insurance rates, fuel costs, hourly labor rates, and the like.

A landscape company's calculation of a recovery markup is contingent upon its primary source of revenue. In contrast to the previous nursery example in which the recovery markup was based on material sales, landscape companies recover their overhead with a labor markup or a combination markup on labor and materials (dual overhead rate). The proportion of labor and material costs associated with a job will determine which markup method is used.

■ Labor Markup

An income statement profile of a landscape maintenance company is illustrated in Figure 3-4. With labor as the predominant direct cost factor, the major portion of overhead expenses are therefore labor related. These costs range from uniform costs to payroll taxes, health insurance, vacation leave, equipment maintenance, sales department salaries and expenses, professional development, and administrative salaries and expenses.

The formula for calculating the labor markup is:

$$\text{Labor overhead markup} = \text{Overhead/Direct labor} + \text{Labor burden}$$
$$= \$600,000/(\$450,000 + \$45,000)$$
$$= 121\%$$

labor burden

costs associated with state and federal payroll taxes and worker's compensation insurance.

Determining the company's hourly selling price for a laborer (Figure 3-5) begins with adding **labor burden,** the costs associated with state and federal payroll taxes and worker's compensation insurance, to the base hourly rate, then applying the overhead markup, and finally adding the desired profit markup. Note that charging any less than $19.89 per hour will result in a loss, since the company will not recover the total costs associated with supporting that labor. The $10.89 amount may seem disproportionate to the hourly rate until you take into consideration what is included in the

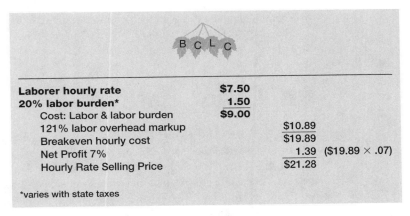

Earned revenue	$1,500,000	
Income Statement		
Net sales	100%	
Direct job costs		
Direct labor	30%	$450,000
Labor burden	3%	45,000
Material	15%	225,000
Subcontractors	5%	75,000
Total Direct Costs	53%	$795,000
Gross margin	47%	705,000
Overhead expenses	40%	600,000
Net Profit	7%	105,000

Figure 3-4   Bradco Landscape Company Income Statement

Laborer hourly rate	**$7.50**	
20% labor burden*	**1.50**	
Cost: Labor & labor burden	**$9.00**	
121% labor overhead markup	$10.89	
Breakeven hourly cost	$19.89	
Net Profit 7%	1.39	($19.89 × .07)
Hourly Rate Selling Price	$21.28	

*varies with state taxes

Figure 3-5   Bradco Landscape Company Labor Hourly Rate Calculation

labor overhead: uniform rental, sick day compensation, general liability insurance, hand tools, medical insurance, holiday and annual leave compensation, supervision, and in some cases pension plan contributions.

■ Dual Overhead Rate Method

Overhead recovery calculated individually for labor and materials is appropriate if the sales of a landscape company are dominated by either one or the other. But what about design/build companies that have a significant amount of sales both in materials and

POTOMAC LANDSCAPE		
Earned revenue	$3,000,000	100%
Direct costs		
Materials	$ 900,000	30%
Labor and labor burden	$ 600,000	20%
Subcontracts	$ 150,000	5%
Other	$ 30,000	1%
Total Direct Costs	$1,680,000	56%
Gross margin	$1,320,000	44%
Overhead expenses	$1,050,000	35%
Net Profit	$ 270,000	9%

Figure 3-6   Potomac Landscape Company

in labor? This question was posed to a think tank at the Fails Management Institute approximately thirty years ago. Dr. Fails, Frank Ross, and colleagues of North Carolina State University pondered the question posed by the landscape industry and ultimately came up with a solution. That solution was the **dual overhead rate method,** which calculates overhead recovery based on the ratio of material to labor costs.

dual overhead rate method
calculates overhead recovery based on the ratio of material to labor costs.

The calculation of a dual overhead rate begins with establishing a materials to labor ratio based on direct costs projected in the company's income statement. An example of an abbreviated income statement projection for a design/build landscape business is presented in Figure 3-6.

materials to labor ratio
calculated by dividing the total material costs by the total labor and labor burden costs.

The **materials to labor ratio** is calculated by dividing the total material direct costs by the total labor and labor burden costs:

$$\text{Materials/labor ratio} = \$900,000/\$600,000 = 1.5/1$$

This ratio is indicative of the proportions of Potomac Landscape's project expenditures allocated to materials and labor. Based on this projection, Potomac can anticipate that for every dollar of production labor there will be a corresponding expenditure of $1.50 for materials.

Determination of this ratio provides a basis for the Dual Overhead Rate Method (DORM) to allocate overhead costs proportionally for those expenses that support materials versus labor. As the M/L ratio increases, the DORM allocates a greater proportion of the overhead costs to materials, and as it decreases, the allocation amount is increased on the labor side.

The next step in the dual overhead rate calculation requires an overhead weighting factor. This factor is obtained by referring to the chart of overhead weighting factors (developed by Dr. Emol Fails) in Figure 3-7. Potomac Landscape's M/L ratio of 1.5 has an overhead weighting factor of 2.79. If an M/L ratio falls between two factors, e.g., 1.53, it is rounded off to the nearest M/L ratio, in this case 1.55. The weighting

| | | M/L—Materials to labor ratio | | | | | |
| | | X—Overhead weighting factors | | | | | |

M/L	X	M/L	X	M/L	X	M/L	X
0.00	1.80	1.00	2.46	2.00	3.13	4.00	4.42
0.05	1.84	1.05	2.49	2.10	3.19	4.20	4.54
0.10	1.88	1.10	2.53	2.20	3.26	4.40	4.66
0.15	1.91	1.15	2.56	2.30	3.33	4.60	4.77
0.20	1.95	1.20	2.59	2.40	3.39	4.80	4.88
0.25	1.98	1.25	2.62	2.50	3.46	5.00	5.00
0.30	2.01	1.30	2.66	2.60	3.53	5.20	5.10
0.35	2.04	1.35	2.69	2.70	3.59	5.40	5.21
0.40	2.07	1.40	2.72	2.80	3.66	5.60	5.31
0.45	2.10	1.45	2.75	2.90	3.72	5.80	5.41
0.50	2.13	1.50	2.79	3.00	3.79	6.00	5.51
0.55	2.16	1.55	2.82	3.10	3.85	6.30	5.65
0.60	2.20	1.60	2.86	3.20	3.92	6.70	5.83
0.65	2.23	1.65	2.90	3.30	3.98	7.00	5.96
0.70	2.26	1.70	2.93	3.40	4.05	7.50	6.15
0.75	2.30	1.75	2.96	3.50	4.11	8.00	6.35
0.80	2.33	1.80	2.99	3.60	4.17	8.50	6.52
0.85	2.36	1.85	3.03	3.70	4.23	9.00	6.68
0.90	2.39	1.90	3.06	3.80	4.30	9.50	6.82
0.95	2.43	1.95	3.09	3.90	4.36	10.00	6.95

Figure 3-7   Overhead Weighting Factors

Source: Pricing for the Green Industry, Frank H. Ross, Ross/Payne & Associates, 2nd edition, © 1997, Professional Landcare Network, Herndon, VA.

factor (X) is the key component in the dual overhead rate formula that determines the distribution of overhead to materials and labor.

DUAL RATE FORMULAS

The overhead weight factor, labor and burden costs, and material costs are the components of the formulas for calculating the markup on materials and the overhead markup on labor.

Potomac Landscape Company

Labor and labor burden costs	$600,000
Material costs	$900,000
Overhead costs	$1,050,000

Overhead markup on material = Overhead /(X)(Labor and Burden) + Material

$1,050,000/(2.79)($600,000) + $900,000 = $1,050,000/2,574,000 = 41%

Overhead markup on labor = (X)Overhead/(X)(Labor and Burden) + Material
(2.79)($1.050,000)/(2.79)($600,000) + $900,000 = $2,929,500/2,574,000 = 114%

The only difference between the two formulas is the additional weight factor that is applied to the labor markup. In this example, the labor and labor burden are weighted an additional 2.79 than the material costs. The basis for application of the additional weight factor to labor and labor burden is to account for the greater portion of overhead costs associated with labor versus materials. Some of the larger overhead expenses that support labor include:

Indirect labor—nonbillable labor compensation, e.g., vacation, sick leave, downtime associated with loading and unloading, picking up material, equipment breakdowns, and so forth.

Payroll taxes

Communications—walkie-talkies, cell phones

Liability insurance—vehicles and equipment

Sales expenses—salaries and salary burden

Administrative expenses—payroll, human resources, professional development

The following calculation validates that the calculated markups will recover all of the overhead expenses that are applied to the budgeted costs for labor and materials:

Total labor and labor burden × Labor markup = Labor overhead recovery
$600,000 × 114% = $684,000
Total material × Material markup = Material overhead recovery
$900,000 × 41% = $369,000
Labor overhead recovery + Material overhead recovery = Total overhead
$684,000 + $369,000 = $1,053,000

The management of the Potomac Landscape Company would be very satisfied with the results of the dual overhead rate markups, since the variance on the plus side is within $3 of the projected annual overhead of $1,050,000.

The following summarizes the application of the three markups methods discussed:

Material markup—used by companies whose sales are primarily materials, e.g., retail and wholesale nurseries

Labor markup—used by landscape companies or divisions whose sales are dominated by labor, e.g., maintenance, snowplowing, pressure washing, and so forth.

Dual rate overhead—applicable to installation jobs that are primarily materials oriented or having comparable amounts of materials and labor.

Design/build companies and installation divisions are examples of companies for which the DORM would be effective in overhead recovery. One of the major criticisms of the DORM method is that it addresses the labor and materials ratio the same throughout the year, based upon the percentage of sales budget projections.

The above methods are just a few examples of how overhead recovery can be calculated. There are several other methods that are used in the landscape industry, such as MORS (Multiple Overhead Recovery System) and OPPH (Overhead and Profit per Hour). Detailed discussions of these and other methods are found in *How to Price Landscape and Irrigation Projects,* by James Huston (Smith, Huston, Inc.). All are built on the premise that of having accurate financial information and budget projections. The key to overhead recovery is knowing what percentage of overhead is associated with specific direct costs.

Companies that have been in business for several years have a financial database that provides a documented history of cost percentages and overhead costs for individual jobs and collectively for their divisions. These percentages may be consistent from year to year if the company is engaged in similar contracts, for example, maintenance or irrigation, or the percentages may vary if the company is engaged in bidding commercial installation contracts. The latter is much more variable due to site conditions, installation components, wage scales, and subcontractors.

The most reliable overhead recovery system is one that is developed internally with a company's financial database as its foundation. A company may use an MORS or dual rate overhead method as the infrastructure of its system with modifications that address specific job situations, such as amount of labor, labor burden, equipment, and materials. Just as with accounting software programs and suits, overhead recovery systems are not perfect fits off the rack.

■ Equipment Pricing Structure

The previous pricing discussion dealt with recovering overhead expenses associated with the direct costs of materials and labor. This was achieved by applying markup methods on the basis of the amount of materials or labor that were associated with the revenues generated.

Another important overhead expense recovery pertains to the equipment employed by landscape companies. The landscape industry, in addition to being labor intensive, is also equipment intensive. Equipment ranging from lawn mowers to backhoes and trenchers comprise a significant portion of a company's fixed assets and overhead expenses. Associated with such equipment is the initial capital cost and maintenance costs. In order to recover these costs, a pricing structure needs to be established for each piece of motorized equipment, including trucks. Depending on how much equipment is used on a job, landscape companies expense it as either a direct cost or an overhead expense. The following examples illustrate the process involved in establishing hourly equipment rates.

The primary cost factor components for pricing equipment at hourly rates are:

1. Acquisition cost per hour (CPH)
   Purchase price (PP) (including taxes and registration fees)
   Loan interest (LI) (duration of the loan)

1. Acquisition cost per hour

   Purchase price: $35,000 (inclusive of taxes and registration fees)

   Loan interest: $35,000 × 4 × .06/2 = $4,200

   Purchase price × years of payments × interest rate

   One-half of loan term (2 years), based on equal monthly payments leaving an outstanding principal loan balance for one-half the period

   Trade-in value: $20,000

   Lifetime hours: 40 hours × 52 weeks × 4 years = 8,320

   Acquisition CPH = $35,000 + $4,200 − $20,000/8,320 hours = $2.31

$$ACPH = PP + LI - TV/LH$$

2. Maintenance cost per hour

License fees (4 years × $150)	600
Insurance ($1,500/year × 4 years)	6,000
Lube, oil, filters (20 × $40)	800
Brake service and replacements (3 × $400)	1,200
Clutch service and replacement (2 × $500)	1,000
Smog certification (2 × $60)	120
Tires (2 sets × $600)	1,200
Miscellaneous maintenance (batteries, etc.)	800
Engine replacement (1/3 vehicles $3,500/3)	1,167
Total	$12,887

   Maintenance CPH = $12,887/8,320 hours = $1.55

$$MCPH = MC/LH$$

3. Fuel cost per hour

   Fuel cost per gallon/miles per gallon × miles driven per day/8 hours

   Fuel CPH = $2.00/15 mpg × 75 miles/8 hours = $1.22

$$FCPH = CPG/MPG \times M/H$$

4. Crew cab truck total cost per hour = $2.31 APH + $1.55 MCPH + $1.22 FCPH
   = $5.08

Figure 3-8   Equipment Pricing: Crew Cab Pickup Truck

   Trade-in value (TV)
   Lifetime hours (LH)

2. Maintenance cost per hour (lifetime projected costs)

3. Fuel cost per hour

4. Total equipment cost per hour

Trucks are collectively the most costly equipment items among a landscape company's fixed assets. They are used by supervisors and crew leaders to transport crews and materials as well as by account managers whose daily travel may entail site estimates, inspections, contract renewals, job supervision, and sales presentations. Figure 3-8 calculates an hourly cost that would be charged for every hour that a crew cab pickup truck is on a job.

As is evident from the calculation in Figure 3-8, the hourly rate recovers a portion of all the costs associated with the vehicle. Contrasting the application of this cost recovery method to a mileage assessment method illustrates the importance of its implementation.

Mileage Assessment Method

Job A Mileage	Mileage Rate	Duration
30 miles	$.34/mile	8 hours
	Mileage cost assessment = $.34 × 30 = $10.54	
	Hourly rate assessment = $5.08 × 8 = $40.64	

The above example shows that a company that uses the mileage assessment method is inadequately covering the costs associated with purchasing, maintaining, and operating this vehicle. The cost difference increases exponentially with the number of crew cab trucks and the total mileage logged on a daily basis. Rather than include the truck costs as a direct cost, many companies will calculate it into an equipment line under overhead expenses.

Every piece of equipment has an hourly rate established using the same pricing components. These hourly rates are coded for each piece of equipment and incorporated into estimates for landscape contracts either as direct or overhead costs.

Companies can obtain equipment production rates, lifetime hours, and maintenance costs from owner's manuals and industry publications, such as *Labor and Equipment Production Times for Landscape Construction*, Vander Koori and Associates, Inc., Littleton, Colorado.

■ Summary

The construction of a pricing structure requires the use of two financial tools that were introduced in the previous two chapters. Those tools are the chart of accounts, which delineates between costs associated with what is sold (direct costs), the costs associated with supporting the sale (overhead), and the budget, which projects those costs as a percentage of annual sales.

What are the pricing components and what is their significance to price determination?

The pricing components consist of:

- Direct costs—labor, labor burden, materials, equipment, subcontractors. These are the primary cost factors associated with job production. A pricing structure is built on the percentage of production revenues.
- Overhead costs—administrative salaries, equipment maintenance, sales salaries, advertising, uniform rentals, professional development. These and other costs that support production are included in pricing as a percentage of the direct cost expenses.

- Profit—capital for growth, retirement of debt, fixed asset purchases, excess compensation, and income tax liabilities. A percentage of profit based on budget projections is calculated into the selling price.

How does the pricing formula apply to the landscape industry?

The pricing formula, direct costs + overhead + profit = selling price, is applicable to all sectors of the landscape industry. Computation of the pricing components varies based on the mix of labor, materials, and equipment.

How are hourly rates determined for labor and equipment?

Hourly labor rates are determined by:

- Adding a percentage of labor burden to the base hourly rate
- Adding a markup for labor overhead
- Adding a profit percentage

Equipment hourly rates are determined by:

- Calculating an acquisition cost per hour
- Calculating a maintenance cost per hour
- Calculating fuel cost per hour
- Adding ACPH + MCPH + FCPH

How is markup calculated for labor and materials?

Markups for labor and materials enable companies to recover overhead expenses associated with these direct costs. Labor markup is determined by:

- Determining annual costs for overhead and direct labor and labor burden
- Dividing overhead costs by labor and labor burden costs,
  overhead ÷ labor + labor burden

Material markup is determined by:

- Determining annual costs for overhead and materials
- Dividing overhead costs by material cost, overhead costs/material costs

How is dual overhead recovery markup calculated and where is it applicable?

The dual overhead recovery method is applicable to installation jobs in which the ratio of materials to labor varies. It calculates overhead markup based on the ratio of materials to labor and a weighting factor that equates to the respective ratio. The dual overhead recovery is calculated by:

- Determining annual costs for labor and labor burden
- Determining annual costs for material
- Determining annual costs for overhead

  1. Calculating the ratio of materials to labor, materials ÷ labor
  2. Determining the weighting factor for the respective ratio

3. Calculating the labor markup,
   (weighting factor) overhead ÷ (weighting factor) labor + labor burden

4. Calculating the material markup,
   overhead ÷ (weighting factor) (labor + labor burden) + material

■ Knowledge Application

1. Buffalo Grove Nursery has annual material costs of $550,000 and overhead costs of $350,000. BGN's projected net profit is 10%.

   a. Calculate the overhead markup for materials.

   b. Calculate the breakeven price for a $750 maple tree.

   c. Calculate the selling price for the maple tree.

2. a. Give three landscape industry examples of dual rate overhead applications.

   b. Why would the DORM method be preferred over individual material and labor markup methods?

3. Based on the financial information that follows:

   a. Calculate the breakeven hourly price.

   b. Calculate the hourly rate selling price.

Overhead costs	$525,000
Labor and labor burden	$350,000
Crew base hourly rate	$8.50
Labor burden base percent	$28%
Projected profit	10%

4. a. Which of the pricing components do you feel has the greatest impact on a company's competitive pricing structure?

   b. Give examples of how companies can reduce direct costs.

Estimating

CHAPTER OBJECTIVES

To gain an understanding of:

1. The estimating system

2. Estimating maintenance jobs

3. Estimating installation jobs

4. Distinguishing between indirect and direct costs

5. The interrelationship between the estimating system and job cost management

By definition, an **estimate** is an approximation or an educated guess. The latter definition is a more accurate depiction of a landscape estimate since it is based on a company's financial database. Once compiled, an estimate is reviewed by management and adjustments are made before a **bid** is submitted representing the total job price. The bid is presented to the client with an accompanying contract that specifies the materials and services that will be provided. There are two distinct contract situations, one that is negotiated, e.g., for a residential client, and one that is not negotiated, e.g., for a commercial client. In a negotiated contract situation, the landscape contractor and client concur on the services and materials that will be provided for a specific price. Bids presented with commercial contracts for maintenance and construction are often competing with other contractor submittals. In these situations, all the bids are based upon the same specifications regarding services and materials that will be provided.

Landscape estimators determine what it takes to complete the job. They estimate all the costs associated with materials, labor, and equipment and then calculate the overhead and profit to compile a bid representing the job selling price. The company's financial history, budget projections, and cost structure provide the estimator with the cost figures required for estimating the selling price formula:

$$\text{Direct Costs} \quad + \quad \text{Overhead} \quad + \quad \text{Profit} = \text{Selling Price}$$

Estimator input   Budget Projections

                 Financial history

KEY TERMS

assembly

bid

contingency clause

crew average wage

digitizer

estimate

landscape estimators

site preparation

take-offs

time and materials
     estimate

estimate
an educated guess or approximation based on a company's financial database.

bid
the total job price presented to a client.

landscape estimators
estimate all the direct costs associated with job production.

■ Estimator's Responsibilities

Landscape contracting estimators have the responsibility of determining quantities of material and hours of labor associated with installation and maintenance jobs. Their determination is based on site analysis, communication with the account managers, and the specifications stipulated in the contracts. Specifications refer to what services are to be provided, e.g., a maintenance estimate would include mowing, seasonal color installation, pruning, fertilizing, and herbicide and pesticide applications, while a construction estimate might include deck construction, retaining walls, water features, and plant installations.

In both maintenance and construction estimates, the estimator needs to determine square footage for the designated areas addressed in the contract. Job site measurements are made either with digitized measuring wheels, which calibrate lineal distance on job sites, or in the case of new construction, with a **digitizer,** which is an electronic instrument that transmits the data to software estimating programs, engineering scales, or planimeters (manual take-off instruments) to determine the square footage from blueprints. Companies that use AutoCAD software use the client's CAD drawings to compute the respective lineal or area measurements.

digitizer

an electronic instrument that transmits measurements from blueprints into software estimating programs.

When blueprints or landscape plans are used, the estimator makes what is referred to as **take-offs,** area measurements and quantities. A maintenance estimate would have take-offs pertaining to turf, shrub, and flower bed areas. Landscape construction take-offs determine areas associated with plant and sod installations, hardscape features such as patios and decks, quantities of plant materials, and irrigation system components.

take-offs

area measurements made and quantities taken from blueprints or landscape plans.

The key estimate components compiled by the estimator are:

1. **Direct costs**—all materials at invoice (billed) cost, labor based on production labor and labor burden, subcontractors at cost, and equipment based on cost per hour required to complete the job (some companies may include this cost in overhead expense).

2. **Indirect costs**—costs associated with the job but not required for the specific service or landscape installation. Examples would be permits, bonds, equipment mobilization, supervision time, travel time, silt fences, and so forth.

The remaining portions of the estimate are standardized calculations for recovering overhead, accounting for specific job conditions, and warranties:

Markups—on labor and materials calculated to recover overhead costs. The overhead recovery is in reference to costs associated with labor and materials. A budgeted markup percentage is often used for maintenance estimates in contrast to landscape construction estimates that may calculate markups on an individual job basis due to variations in the proportion of material and labor costs.

Risk factor—a percentage markup added to landscape construction jobs that is included for unanticipated conditions that may result in additional labor or materials. Drainage or compaction on a construction site would be an example, or discovering unmarked utilities or old foundations and footings.

Warranty—a percentage markup of the total job cost, generally 3–5% to cover the costs associated with replacement of materials under warranty.

Sales tax—on all materials used in the job.

Profit—based on the current budgeted amount to meet the company's financial needs in regard to growth projections, retirement of debt, excess compensation, capital expenditures, and fixed asset acquisitions. The dollar amount of profit is calculated as a percentage of the total job cost.

Profit percentages vary for landscape maintenance companies and construction companies depending on their client base, commercial or residential. Another factor considered by construction companies is the competitiveness of a commercial job. A company may be willing to reduce its profit margin depending on the job size and the potential for future jobs with the client or general contractor. A Professional Landcare Network survey of landscape contracting companies (based on 1997 figures) lists profit percentages for maintenance companies with a commercial client base as 10.2% and for those with a residential base as 14.5%. The survey gives the range in profit percentages for landscape construction companies as 7.6% to 15.3%. The higher profit percentages are generally associated with residential construction companies.

The final estimate stipulates:

What is to be done—job production

How many labor hours—job completion

Quantities of materials—per operation

Total production costs

Total selling price

◼ Production Standards

Before a company can generate an estimate, it has to have a database of production standards. These standards are predetermined by tracking the production of crews working on specific maintenance services, plant installation, or construction. The tracking process entails having the crew supervisor's record of production times for all phases of installation and construction operations. These standards are adjusted when practices change due to the introduction of new equipment (e.g., motor-powered bed edger, mulch blowers, leaf vacuums). The information that is compiled will include:

- Area—square footage or lineal feet
- Hours to completion (based on crew size and individual work hours)
- Power equipment production time
- Quantity or size of materials

Once this database is established, an estimating software program can extrapolate the data into the respective production categories.

Examples of production rates are given in Figures 4-1 and 4-2. Although these are actual production figures from the landscape industry, they should not be considered as industry benchmarks, since site conditions vary.

Description	Unit	Qty/Work Hour*	Production Time	Equipment
Site Preparation				
Grading to +/− .1/ft	SF	4–6,000	10–15 min/1000 SF	tractor
Rototilling 6″ depth	SF	1–2,000	40 min/1,000 SF	rototiller
Finish grade	SF	1,000	60 min/1,000 SF	
Planting				
(inclusive of placement to mulch ring preparation)				
Trees				
(box—diameter, balled & burlapped—caliper)				
72″ box	Ea	.125	8 hrs	1 hr backhoe
60″ box /5″ caliper	Ea	.167	6 hrs	.8 hr backhoe
48″ box/4″ caliper	Ea	.25	4 hrs	.5 hr backhoe
24″ box/2″ caliper	Ea	.50	2 hrs	.25 hr backhoe
Trees				
(containers)				
15 gallon	Ea	1.0	1 hr	
5 gallon	Ea	5.0	12 min	
1 gallon	Ea	12–15	4–5 min	
Staking & Guying	3 stakes	2	30 min	
Shrubs				
(balled & burlapped)				
3′	Ea	.75	1.3 hrs	
2′	Ea	1.2	.8 hrs	
1½′	Ea	2–2.5	.33–.5 hrs	
1′	Ea	3–4	15–20 min	
Shrubs				
(containers)				
15 gallon	Ea	1	1 hr	
5 gallon	Ea	4–5	12–15 min	
1 gallon	Ea	12–15	4–5 min	
Ground cover				
2¼″ pots	Flt	1.5–2	30–45 min	
Sod	SF	225–300	20–27 min/100	

Figure 4-1   Plant Installation Production Rates

Source: How to Price Landscape and Irrigation Projects, Smith Huston, Inc., Englewood, CO.
*Production of one worker within a one-hour period.

Service	Equipment	Work Hours	Comments
Mowing*	21″ rotary	1.75 hrs/10,000 SF	Mulching blade
		2.0 hrs/10,000 SF	Collecting clippings
	48″ riding	1.0 hr/32,000 SF	Mulching blade
		1.0 hr/28,000 SF	Collecting clippings 1.6 mph
	60″ mower	1.0 hr/1.25 acres	2.5–3.5 mph
Thatching	Walk behind	4.0 hrs/10,000 SF	
Fertilizing	Rotary spreader	1.0 hr/acre	Non-divided
		1.0 hr/20,000 SF	Residential property
	Drop spreader	1.0 hr/15,000 SF	
Herbicide application	Rotary spreader	1.0 hr/acre	Preemergent
	Sprayer	1.0 hr/15M SF	Postemergent
Hedge trimming	Hedge	.25 hr/80 lineal feet	5.6′ × 5.6′ hedge
		2.5 hr	Cleanup
Bed edging	Power stick edger	.35 hr/100 lineal feet	Inclusive of cleanup
Tree ring edging	Hand	.35 hr/30″ diameter	
		.50 hr/36″–46″ diameter	

Figure 4-2 Maintenance Production Rates*

Source: Guide to Growing a Successful Landscape Maintenance Business, Professional Landcare Network, Herndon, VA, reprinted with permission.
*Production of one worker within a one hour period.

Once a company establishes its production rates, it has a database for estimating the total production hours for each of its operations, for example, planting, mowing, and edging.

The formula for estimating total production hours is:

Total Production Hours = Unit Quantity × Production Standard × Operation Frequency

Examples of production hours estimate for maintenance and installation operations are:

Hedge Trimming: Total Production Hours = 160 ft. × .50 hr × 7 = 560 hours

The production hours estimate for trimming 160 ft. of hedge seven times is 560 hours.

Planting ten 5-gallon shrubs: Total Production Hours = 10 × .25 hr × 1 = 2.5 hrs

The production hours estimate for planting ten 5-gallon shrubs, based on these standards, is two and a half hours.

■ Estimating Procedure

A lot of responsibility lies on the shoulders of estimators. The estimates that they generate provide the foundation for establishing project budgets. The project managers will use their budgets to develop production schedules, which are based on projected costs and hours derived from the estimate.

Regardless of the project manager's management skills and the production efficiency of the crews, the bottom line profit is contingent upon the accuracy of the estimated labor and materials costs. How do estimators ensure the accuracy of their estimates? By becoming familiar with all aspects of the project. This is accomplished by analyzing the site.

SITE ANALYSIS—MAINTENANCE

The estimator assesses the site's landscape status in terms of overall conditions, turf, shrub beds, and trees. This analysis will reveal whether renovation of any of the landscape entities is warranted: bed edging, tree rings, postemergent weed applications, pesticide applications, turf aeration and fertilization, corrective pruning, and so on. This estimate is different from one that is presented for a year-round contract. The basis for a renovation estimate is to elevate the maintenance standards of the property and begin the process of establishing a management program.

A conventional estimate for a maintenance contract would entail estimating services specified by the potential client. The basic services that may be included in the estimate are mowing, trimming, edging, fertilizing, applying chemicals for weed, insect, and disease control, pruning, mulching, removing leaves, and in cold climates removing snow and deicing. An estimating form for such services is illustrated in Figure 4-3.

SITE ANALYSIS—INSTALLATION, DESIGN/BUILD

A thorough analysis is made of the site conditions, soil structure, drainage issues, utilities, construction issues associated with subcontractors, site logistics, and access, verification of blueprint measurements, and designated landscape construction areas. Estimating production hours often is the most challenging part of an estimator's job for design/build projects. Although the company's production rates are accessed through its estimating database, there are unforeseen circumstances associated with new construction sites. Allowances need to be made for delays in site access, for example, if the contract does not allow for compensation through a contract **contingency clause,** which stipulates compensation for unforeseen circumstances—weather or construction site delays. It is also imperative that the estimator thoroughly review the job specifications and architectural plans to ensure that compliance will not cause unusual financial risks, such as installation of a roof garden with inadequate accommodations for drainage and weight.

contingency clause
stipulates compensation for unforeseen circumstances.

REVIEW OF JOB SPECIFICATIONS

Job specifications include such information as the size of materials (e.g., tree caliper, crown diameter) and installation standards (e.g., diameter of planting hole, elevation of root ball above grade, staking system, backfill mix). The specifications accommodate the landscape plans and are provided by the landscape architects. These specifications may be based on industry standards such as those provided by a trade association (e.g., Landscape Contractors Association MD, DC, VA), as well as those that are associated with municipalities. An example of exterior plant installation specifications for tree installation is shown; additional details would be listed for staking or attaching guy wires for support.

- Tree installation (balled and burlapped):
  A. Planting pits should be dug with vertical sides in friable soils or angled outward and scarified in heavy soils.
  B. The depth of the pit should allow for ⅛ of the root ball to be above grade.
  C. There should be a minimum of 9″ between the pit side walls and the root ball.
  D. Percolation tests are required in situations where poor drainage is anticipated. The test involves filling a 12″ × 18″ hole with water and assessing the amount of water remaining after eight hours. If excess water remains, a drainage system is required.
  E. Backfill mix shall consist of ¾ native soil, ¼ organic matter, and organic fertilizer. Soil tests are required to determine if any other additives are necessary.
  F. Remove the burlap from the upper 50% of the root ball and roll it back to the edges of the root ball. Remove all rope or synthetic twine from the entire root ball.
  G. Thoroughly mix the backfill and fill 50% of the tree pit, lightly tamping the mix during the process. Fill the remainder of the pit with the balance of the mix.
  H. Leave the top of the root ball exposed.
  I. Use the mix to form a saucer around the root ball.
  J. Mulch the top of the root ball, not to exceed a 3″ depth. Taper the mulch away from the base of the trunk.
  K. Fill the saucer with water and follow with more water if the conditions are dry.

COMPILATION

The *compilation* of an estimate involves the determination of:

I. *Direct costs* associated with providing the maintenance service or construction phase:

Material at wholesale cost

crew average wage
calculated by dividing the total hourly crew wages by the number of crew members.

Labor as actual hours, **crew average wage** (CAW) or at an hourly production wage rate

Foreman	$12.50
Leadman	9.00
Laborer	7.50
Laborer	7.50
	$36.50

$$CAW = \$36.50/4 = \$9.12$$

Labor burden as a percent of the hourly wage

Federal income tax
Social Security tax
Medicare
Federal unemployment tax
State income tax
State unemployment tax
Workers' compensation insurance
Equipment costs based on hours of use and assessed cost per hour
Subcontractors at actual cost

II. *Indirect costs,* encompassing those items necessary for production completion but not directly involved in the actual production phase. Silt fences would be an example in a construction project. Labor associated with loading and unloading materials and equipment is another example. Think of indirect costs in the same vein as overhead, which is the umbrella for everything that is necessary to support the delivery of maintenance service or construction product. Other examples of indirect costs include uniforms, permits, soil tests, temporary fencing, dump fees, travel time, supervisor hours (if not accounted for in direct labor), and watering plants in the staging (holding) area.

III. *Markups,* percentage increases applied to specific costs for recovery of overhead costs. They are applied to:

Labor to recover costs associated with supporting labor:

Vacation compensation
Sick leave compensation
Holiday compensation
Liability insurance
Medical insurance
Pension plan
Training
Uniforms
Small tools

Materials to recover overhead costs associated with handling and maintenance, loading and unloading

IV. *Profit,* a percentage of the total job cost

Profit = Breakeven cost* × percentage complement**

Profit percentage complement is derived from dividing the desired profit percentage (10%) by 100% − the desired percentage, 10%)

---

*Direct costs + overhead markup
**Percentage complement = 10%/100% − 10% = .1111%

Example:

Breakeven job cost = $12,000
Profit = $12,000 × .1111 = $1,333.20
Selling price = $12,000 + $1,333.20 = $13,333.20
Profit = $13,333.20/$1,333.20 = 10%

This method of profit calculation is more accurate than determining profit by multiplying the desired percentage times the breakeven cost. For example,

$12,000 × 10% = $1,200
Selling price = $12,000 + $1,200 = $13,200
Profit = $1,200/$13,200 = 9.09%

Typical net profits in the landscape industry are 6–10% for maintenance commercial jobs, 3–5% for commercial bid construction, and 15–20% for residential design/build projects. These percentages are contingent upon several factors:

1. Job size—smaller profit percentage with larger commercial jobs

2. Production efficiency—job cost management

3. Negotiated vs. bid contracts—generally larger profit percentages with negotiated contracts

4. Market competition

5. Weather/construction delays—resulting in labor production overruns

6. Bottom line—what the company needs for profit, growth, employment compensation, retiring debt

Travel time is also an important factor in estimating along with labor, materials and equipment. This information is not only important when costing the job, but it also provides a basis on which managers can schedule the jobs. Scheduling allocates work hours and equipment on a daily basis from job initiation to completion. This allocation will apply to phases of an installation project as well as services provided in a maintenance contract.

Estimate formats are presented in Figures 4-3 and 4-4 for maintenance and installation estimates, respectively. The maintenance estimate determines the hours of service required based on job site area measurements. The hours of service are based on the company's production standards.

assembly
a compilation of operations associated with a specific phase of a contract.

The landscape construction format (Figure 4-4) illustrates the components of a plant installation assembly. An **assembly** represents a compilation of operations associated with a specific phase of the landscape construction contract.

site preparation
may included grading, soil amelioration, and demolition.

Another example of landscape construction assembly is **site preparation.** This process includes soil amelioration, which incorporates soil amendments into the native soil, grading, and demolition, which may include removal of plant materials or hardscape features such as walkways, driveways, or old patios.

Client: _____ Location: _____

Property Manager: _____ Contract Period: _____

Telephone: _____ e-mail: _____

Maintenance Services	Hrs./Service Frequency	Service Hours	Labor	Cost/Hour	Total Cost
Turf					
Mowing, trimming, edging					
Fertilizing					
Herbicides					
Preemergent					
Postemergent					
Insecticides					
Shrubs					
Pruning					
Corrective					
Rejuvenation					
Fertilizing					
Herbicides					
Preemergent					
Postemergent					
Insecticides					
Fungicides					
Mulching					
Flowerbeds					
Herbicides					
Fungicides					
Insecticides					
Fertilizing					
Mulching					
Trees					
Pruning					
Corrective (up to 15′)					
Fertilizing					
Insecticide					
Other					
Leaf removal					
Deicing					

Figure 4-3 Landscape Maintenance Estimate Form

Materials	Quantity	Unit Cost	Total Cost
Herbicides Preemergent			
Postemergent			
Fungicides			
Insecticides			
Fertilizers			
Mulch			
Other Surfactant			
Dye marker			
Deicer			
Growth retardant			

Total labor cost		_____
Total material cost		_____
Labor markup		_____
Material markup		_____
Sales tax		_____
Total estimated cost		_____

Figure 4-3   (continued)

Project Number	Assembly	Takeoff Quantity	Production Rate	Labor Hours	Labor Cost/Hr	Labor Cost
123	**Planting Trees** Platanus xacerifolia 'Bloodgood'	54–5"	6 hr/ea with equip.	324 hr	13.79	4,467.96
	Preemergent	3.91 lb				
	Fertilizer	35.10 lbs				
	Mulch rings	2.36 cyd	1.18cyd/hr	2.00 hr	13.79	27.60
	Tree stakes (36")	162	6.67 ea/hr	24.30	13.79	335.10
	Hose Wire	162 ft 1,620 ft				
	Backfill	8.10 cyd				

Project Number	Assembly	Material Cost/Unit	Material Cost	Total Cost
123	**Planting Trees** Platanus xacerifolia 'Bloodgood'	540.00	29,160	33,627.96
	Preemergent	.77/lb	3.01	3.00
	Fertilizer	.07/lb	2.53	3.00
	Mulch rings	12.50 cyd	29.44	57.00
	Tree stakes (36")	. 58 ea	93.96	429.00
	Hose Wire	.30/ft .04/ft	48.60 64.80	49.00 65.00
	Backfill	8.50/cyd	68.85	69.00

Estimate totals: Labor _____

Materials _____

Travel time _____

Supervisor cost _____

Material tax _____

Extra watering time _____

Freight–plants _____

Labor overhead markup _____

Material overhead markup _____

Subcontractors _____

Subtotal _____

Profit _____

Total Estimate _____

Figure 4-4 Landscape Construction Estimate Format

Benefits: Increases consistency and accuracy
Increases bid volume
Provides data for job costing
Gives flexibility in accounting interfacing
Provides database for generating reports
Gives immediate access to job analysis

Essential: Supports staff with accurate and prompt data entry
Updates data: Wages—crew average wage
Unit material costs
Equipment hourly rates
Overhead costs

Figure 4-5 Computerized Estimating

■ Computer System Interface

There are many computerized estimating programs available to the landscape industry. An estimating system increases the efficiency of generating estimates and the accuracy of those estimates. Data entry includes the job site measurements, quantities, and services/operations. The estimating program generates the costs and production rates from its database and adds in the markups and profit. The database is updated on a regular basis to account for increases in labor costs, labor burden, and material costs. The benefits of a computerized estimating system are enumerated in Figure 4-5.

■ Time and Materials Estimates

time and materials estimate
generated for landscape operations that were not specified in the original contract.

It is fairly common for landscape contractors to engage in work that was not included in the original contract. This situation may occur with a maintenance contract (e.g., one time leaf removal), construction contract (e.g., installation of a paved walkway), or design/build contract (e.g., construction of a water feature). In these instances the contractors would bid the additional work on a **time and materials** basis. As the name implies, this estimate is based on the labor and material costs required to complete the landscape operation. The pricing process is the same as in other estimates, but a portion of overhead is billed as a direct cost with labor. The majority of the overhead in question is in support of the direct labor, such as project management, uniform expense, and small tools. The reason for direct billing some of the overhead is that this lowers the markup for recovery of overhead, since a portion is being billed as a direct expense. A lower markup enables a contractor to be in a more competitive position to secure the additional work. Markups are calculated as previously discussed based on the proportion of materials and labor in the job.

Labor Cost Components	Supervisor	Laborer
Base hourly rate	$12.00	$ 6.50
Vacation compensation	.51	.26
Holiday compensation	.41	.12
Sick leave	.16	.07
Social Security tax	1.00	.51
Federal unemployment tax	.11	.06
State unemployment tax	.92	.47
Workers' compensation tax	.61	.31
General liability insurance	.24	.13
Medical insurance	.72	.68
Pension plan	.48	.27
Employee training	.39	.36
Uniform	.21	.14
Small tools	.58	.54
Total Direct Labor Costs	$18.34	$10.42

Figure 4-6   Time and Materials Hourly Rate Components*

Source: Pricing for the Green Industry, 2nd edition, 1997, Frank Ross, Ross/Payne &
Associates Inc., Barrington, IL.
*Components and their percentage of hourly rate are contingent upon company policies and
state tax rates.

The client and contractor agree on the pricing structure prior to the initiation of the operation. All costs associated with the additional work are listed and direct billed (invoiced). The hourly labor rate is inclusive of labor burden and overhead such as vacation and holiday compensation, sick leave, training, and so on, all of which are calculated as a percentage of the base hourly rate. A $12/hr supervisor with overhead and labor burden may therefore be billed at $18.34 (Figure 4-6).

A time and materials rate sheet is shown in Figure 4-7. The labor rate and materials are specified for the landscape operation.

Estimating is a process involving job site analysis and projection of cost factors associated with job production. It is a process that depends on accessing current financial data from the following resources:

- Accounting system—a database for accessing labor and material costs
- Production standards—time required for landscape operations
- Budget—projected profit requirement, overhead, and direct cost percentages

Billing Information	Job Information
Bill To: __RaeCo General Contractors__	Date of Job Completion: __May 24, 2005__
Address: __3644 Boston Street__	Job Site: __Lamco Corporate Park__
__College Park, MD 20742__	Job #: __43215__
Phone: __(301) 405-7834__	Contact Person: __Brad Passat__

Estimated Hours	Actual Hours	Quantity	Description	Unit Cost/Hr	Total Cost
2.0			Front-end loader	$65	
5.0			Labor	$30	
2.0			Supervisor	$45	
4.0			Equipment operator	$35	
		10 cyd	Hardwood mulch	$25/cyd	

Figure 4-7   Time and Materials Rate Sheet

■ Summary

What is an estimating system?

An estimating system generates a price for all of the costs associated with the production of landscape operations. It uses the company's financial database to determine hourly production rates, overhead markups, and profit. The total estimated price is the bid that is submitted to the client. The estimate also serves as a job cost budget.

How are maintenance jobs estimated?

Maintenance jobs are estimated on the basis of the frequency of specified landscape services. Job site area measurements determine the labor hours required to perform the services. Company production rates provide the basis for estimating the hourly labor costs for the maintenance services. Material costs are estimated based on the quantity used. Overhead markups and profit are derived from budget projections.

How are installation jobs estimated?

Installation jobs are estimated on quantity and area measurements derived from landscape plans and/or job sites. Assemblies compile the components of the installation production. Production rates are derived from the estimating database along with hourly cost rates, overhead markups, and profit. Large commercial installation jobs incorporate contingency fees for unforeseen circumstances and a risk factor percentage for unexpected site conditions.

What is the distinction between direct costs and indirect costs?

Direct costs are all costs associated with job production. These costs include labor, labor burden, materials, and equipment. Indirect costs are related to jobs but are not production oriented. Some indirect costs include job permits, travel time, warranty expenses, small tools, and uniform expense.

What is the relationship between the estimating system and job cost management?

Estimates project all costs associated with landscape operations. They also establish the number of hours required to produce all aspects of the operations. An estimate therefore becomes the budget for managing landscape jobs. Managers are able to incorporate the projected costs into daily and weekly management reports for field supervisors.

■ Knowledge Application

1. What can an estimator do to ensure that the final estimate is an accurate assessment of the production costs?
2. How would you establish production standards for mowing residential properties?
3. Using the production rate tables in Figures 4-1 and 4-2, calculate the total production hours for:
   a. Power stick edging, 3,000 SF, 24 weeks
   b. Grading 5,000 SF with a tractor
   c. Planting 10 flats of 2¼″ ground cover
4. Differentiate between negotiated and non-negotiated contracts in terms of job estimates.

Financial Management

CHAPTER OBJECTIVES

To gain an understanding of:

1. The components of balance sheets and income statements

2. The financial implications of balance sheets and income statements

3. Job cost management systems

4. Job cost reporting

5. Management of profit centers (divisions/departments)

6. Contract management responsibilities

KEY TERMS

balance sheet

cash flow report

financial management

job cost management

owner's equity

purchase order

retainage

solvency

work in progress
    schedule

The preceding chapters laid the foundation for the subject of this chapter. A financial library was established with categorized accounts for every financial transaction that occurs in a company. This reference library was used to extrapolate information for the development of budgets, pricing structures, and estimating systems. All of these financial elements are building blocks for financial management. Budgets provide road maps for projected revenue and expenses, pricing structures encapsulate direct and overhead costs, and estimating systems incorporate information from both to generate profitable sales.

A financial reporting system that interfaces with all of the business operations enables management to monitor the pulse of the company.

> "Financial information is the heart that keeps competitive companies beating. Accounting keeps the heartbeat stable."

Compilation of the financial information into two key reports, the balance sheet and the income statement, provides management with heart monitors. Equally if not more important than monitoring the heart is monitoring the pulse. This is accomplished with a cash flow report that determines whether the blood is flowing upstream or downstream and at what rate. All of these financial reports are important tools management uses to ensure that a company functions in a profitable mode. The financial information generated in these reports enables analysis and identification of costs that are exceeding budget projections and the ability of the company to meet its financial obligations.

■ Balance Sheet

balance sheet

lists a company's assets and liabilities; the ratio of these two entities indicates a company's financial stability.

solvency

a company's ability to meet its financial obligations.

The **balance sheet** is the most important document produced by an accounting system. It indicates the financial status of a business at a specified date and establishes the company's **solvency,** or its ability to meet its financial obligations. As the name implies, the balance sheet reflects a balance between financial entities, assets and liabilities. The balance sheet is indicative of a company's financial status. It represents the company's net worth and its ability to meet its financial obligations.

The components of a company's balance sheet include assets and liabilities. Assets represent everything of economic value, which includes current and fixed assets:

Current assets—include cash in bank accounts, short-term investments, money market accounts, and any other investments or assets that can be converted to cash quickly, such as inventory and securities. Inventory items, whether plant materials, chemicals, or hardscape materials, represent items that haven't been sold. Their value is assessed at wholesale cost.

Accounts receivable—represent revenues earned and billed but not collected. They remain categorized as assets until they exceed a certain number of days outstanding, generally more than ninety days. Those accounts that remain outstanding are listed as bad debt.

Fixed assets—are of a more permanent nature: buildings, equipment, and real estate, all of which have value but are not intended for liquidation. The fixed assets all have an annual depreciation (tax allowance) that is deducted from their value.

Liabilities are financial obligations:

Current liabilities—are those that are due within a year or less: vendor invoices, taxes.

Account payables—are monies owed to vendors, utilities, and other expense sources associated with operational expenses.

Accrued taxes and salaries—are those that have not been paid at the date the balance sheet is generated.

Long-term liabilities—are those that are due beyond a year: e.g., mortgages, vehicle loans.

owner's equity

represents the amount of money that remains after liabilities are subtracted from assets.

Owner's equity represents the amount of money that remains after liabilities are subtracted from assets.

CARRIECO NURSERY

Vendor Invoice

Invoice 4/04/05
Shipment No. 35467

BradCo Landscape Company
2634 Baltimore Avenue
College Park, MD 20742

Quantity	Description	Unit Cost	Total Cost
5	Quercus alba 2 1/2" diam.	$120	$600
10	Betula nigra 8' ht. clump	75	750
35	Magnolia stellata 8' ht.	170	5,950
125	Stella De Oro 1 gal.	4	500
200	Rudbeckia "Goldsturm" 1 gal.	4	800
		Subtotal	$8,600
		Shipping	860
		Total Cost	$9,460

Vendor Invoices Comprise of Accounts Payable for Purchased Materials and Services

A balance sheet application can be illustrated with a personal finance situation. A couple decides that they want to buy a bigger house and purchase an SUV. First they have to add up their assets: the cash in their bank and checking accounts, stocks, bonds, home equity (difference between mortgage balance and market value), furniture and any other property that has monetary value. Then they subtract the total of all their liabilities—credit card debt, outstanding bills, mortgage balance, and other loan balances—from their total assets. The dollar amount arrived at represents the current

BradCo Landscape Company
March 31, 2004

Assets		
Current assets		
Cash & securities		$ 30,000
Accounts receivable		150,000
Inventory		60,000
Total current assets		$240,000
Fixed assets		
Land		75,000
Building and improvements	$250,000	
Less: Accumulated depreciation	−95,000	155,000
Furniture and fixtures	30,000	
Less: Accumulated depreciation	16,000	14,000
Vehicles and equipment	375,000	
Less: Accumulated depreciation	−165,000	210,000
Total fixed assets		$454,000
Total Assets		$694,000
Liabilities and Owner's Equity		
Liabilities		
Current		
Accounts payable		50,000
Accrued taxes		9,000
Accrued salaries		175,000
Notes payable (due December 2004)		50,000
Total Current Liabilities		$284,000
Long-term liabilities		
Notes payable (due June 2005)		105,000
Total long-term liabilities		$105,000
Total liabilities		$389,000
Owner's Equity		
Common Stock (dividends)		100,000
Retained earnings		205,000
Total owners' equity		305,000
Total liabilities and owners' equity		$694,000

Figure 5-1 Balance Sheet Format

net worth of the couple. This net worth is referred to in business terms as *owner's equity*. The couple's equity will indicate how much liability they can assume with their desired purchases of a new home and an SUV. In principle, this process is analogous to the one used in preparing a company's balance sheet (Figure 5-1).

The balance sheet is based on the fundamental accounting equation:

$$\text{Assets} = \text{Liabilities} + \text{Owner's Equity}$$

The assets are balanced by the liabilities and owner's equity. Liabilities are financial obligations that are paid from current assets.

Personal assets represent current income plus interest, dividends, securities, material property, house, car, furniture, computer, and so on. Monthly liability payments include: mortgages, car loans, utilities, credit card balances, and so forth. These payments are made from current assets or income. The difference between the liabilities and assets represents one's personal net worth or equity. BradCo Landscape Company's owner's equity, $305,000, is the difference between the company's assets and its liabilities ($694,000–$389,000).

Balance sheets are generated on a quarterly basis. They are indicators of the financial health of the company based on the ratio of liabilities to assets. The end-of-year balance sheet generated on December 31 is a reflection on how management performed. This report contains financial information that reflects whether the company was fiscally responsible in managing its short- and long-term liabilities. The indicator of management's performance is the ratio of assets to liabilities. A bank will look at a ratio of 2:1 or at least 1:1 of assets to liabilities as an indication of a company's financial stability and as a qualifying factor for a credit line or loan. In this example, the BradCo Landscape Company is in good financial health for the first quarter of 2004. Its assets ($694,000) are greater than its liabilities ($389,000), so if the business closed its doors tomorrow, it would be able to liquidate its assets and meet all of its financial liabilities.

In further analysis, however, management would note the fact that the current assets ($240,000) are insufficient to meet the current liabilities ($284,000). The concern is that if the company's sales slumped due to weather or contract cancellations, there would be insufficient funds to meet the company's current liability obligations. Management would therefore consider building up a larger cash reserve and ensuring a line of credit in the event of negative cash flow (expenses exceeding revenue). The collections department would also be notified to keep close tabs on accounts receivable, in regard to their current status. Although accounts receivable are assets, there are instances in which accounts become delinquent, and therefore they will be accounted for as bad debt (after ninety days).

To assess financial performance, balance sheets are always compared to past years. This comparison will reflect consistency or inconsistency in the management of assets and liabilities. The balance sheet also reflects the financial impact of a new division/profit center, for example, sports turf maintenance, because of the liabilities that would be associated with its start up expenses.

■■■ Income Statement

In contrast to the balance sheet that reflects a company's overall financial status, an *income statement* reflects the *profit that is earned from current revenue*. The term *income statement* is used interchangeably with *profit and loss statement*. When managers refer to the "bottom line" they are referring to the amount of profit retained from revenues after costs and expenses. The profit figure is reported in the income statement.

The balance sheet reflects a company's financial status within a specific period. The income statement reflects the profitability of a company's business operations within a specific period of time. A balance sheet is a snapshot while an income statement is a motion picture.

This financial report provides a management tool for detecting deviations from the budget. By analyzing income statements, managers can determine what adjustments need to be made to attain their respective budgeted targets.

The annual income statement as shown in Figure 5-2 provides an overall summary of a company's financial performance. This performance can be assessed on the basis of benchmarks achieved in previous years. The percentages, similar to production time standards, provide a means of measuring costs against a baseline. Any cost deviations from the baseline (budget) alerts management to investigate the cause and to make adjustments that will reduce costs to target the budgeted profit goal. In order to achieve this goal, management must be proactive by monitoring weekly and monthly income statements.

Direct costs, which are associated with production, labor, and materials, are the primary focus of the profit center (divisions) income statements. Landscape companies continuously strive for production efficiency to reduce labor, the major constituent of direct costs. The effect of these efforts will be reflected on the income statement. The efficiency factor reflects the amount of time expended to complete production operations. Nonbillable labor is one cost that can be reduced easily, since it is often associated with downtime or nonproductive time. If the labor percentage exceeds the budget, it may be indicative of nonproductivity, which may be associated with delayed crew departures, excessive travel time, or fueling and loading inefficiency. Other factors such as weather and under estimates may also be related to labor budget variances.

Many of the overhead costs are fixed, meaning they will be the same regardless of the sales volume. Such costs include rent, utilities, administrative salaries and advertising expenses. Management of the budgeted percentages will ensure that these costs remain constant, such as insurance premiums and advertising expenses.

The expediency of software accounting systems enables the generation of real time income statements, daily, weekly, and monthly. Management can monitor the bottom line status of the overall company, of individual branches, and of each profit center. Large corporations utilize the Internet to enable regional offices to compare their financial performance against one another.

Think of the income statement as a report card. The company's grade is reflected on the bottom line. A spreadsheet format as shown in Figure 5-3 provides a comparison of current company performance against the budget for the period and year to date. The components of each cost category would be listed and compared to budgeted figures.

Columbia Landscape Maintenance Company
Annual Income Statement, 2004

Sales Volume $580,000

	Percentage of Sales	$
Net Sales	100%	$580,000
Direct Job Costs		
Direct labor	30.0	174,000
Direct labor burden	4.0	23,200
Material costs	16.0	92,800
Subcontractors	5.1	29,580
Other direct costs	1.4	8,120
Total Direct Job Costs	56.5	$327,700
Gross Margin	43.5	252,300
Indirect Overhead		
Indirect labor	0.5	2,900
Equipment rental	1.2	6,960
Fuel & oil	2.7	15,660
Equipment/vehicle insurance	1.0	5,800
Equipment/vehicle maintenance	3.6	20,880
Tools & supplies	0.9	5,220
Miscellaneous	0.5	2,900
Total Indirect Overhead	10.4	$ 60,320
General & Administrative Overhead		
Marketing	0.6	$ 3,480
Depreciation	3.8	22,040
Insurance—medical & life	1.1	6,380
Insurance—Liability	0.8	4,640
Insurance—workers' compensation	1.0	5,800
Office expense	1.3	7,540
Payroll taxes	1.2	6,960
Profit sharing/pension	0.4	2,320
Rent	1.7	9,860
Salaries—officers/owners	8.0	46,400
Salaries—administrative	4.0	23,200
Salaries—sales	0.2	1,160
Communication system	1.3	7,540
Travel & entertainment	0.4	2,320
Utilities	0.4	2,320
Miscellaneous	2.1	12,180
Total General and Administrative Overhead	28.3	$164,140
Net income (profit) before taxes	4.8	$ 27,840
Pretax profit + Owner's salary	12.8	$ 74,240

Figure 5-2   Annual Income Statement

Current Period	Actual		Budget		Variance
	$	%	$	%	
Net Sales					
Direct Job Costs					
Total Direct Costs					
Gross Margin					
Indirect Overhead					
Total Direct Overhead					
General & Admin. Overhead					
Total General & Admin. Overhead					
Net Profit					

Year to Date	Actual		Budget		Variance
	$	%	$	%	
Net Sales					
Direct Job Costs					
Total Direct Costs					
Gross Margin					
Indirect Overhead					
Total Direct Overhead					
General & Admin. Overhead					
Total General & Admin. Overhead					
Net Profit					

Figure 5-3   Income Statement Spreadsheet Format

■ Cash Flow Reports

cash flow report
indicates the cash balance remaining from cash received after expenses are paid.

A **cash flow report** indicates the source and monthly amounts of cash received, the monthly cash disbursements, and the cash balance. Regardless of the sales volume and profit of a company, unless it operates in a positive cash mode, it will be in financial trouble. Companies generate profit and loss statements (income statements), but these don't tell the whole story. On paper, these statements may show that the company is profitable on generated sales, but they don't say how much cash is available to pay bills, salaries, loan payments, and so forth. Profit is just a number on a page until the cash is in the bank.

If cash flow is reduced because of delinquent accounts receivable, late invoicing, or loss of business, a company can find itself financially overextended, in other words, not enough cash is coming in to pay the bills. In other situations, design/build companies can easily go into negative cash flow when working on large projects involving high labor and material costs. These costs are paid in advance of final billing. Commercial installation companies generally receive partial payments based on the percentage of completion of various phases of the job. However, regardless of the partial payments, costs still exceed cash flow from these projects. A company has to be careful not to overcommit to such jobs unless it uses a line of credit or has sufficient cash reserves to finance the upfront costs.

Maintenance contracts are prorated over a twelve-month period. Therefore, companies receive the same amount of cash flow regardless of the season. In the late fall and winter months, production costs are low due to seasonal labor layoffs and reduced labor associated with the services required at that time of year. Therefore, the company is in positive cash flow since the revenues exceed the cash outflows. However, when the spring season begins, material and labor costs rise while the revenues remain constant, thereby causing a negative cash flow. A maintenance company whose fiscal year begins in April will experience negative cash flow for approximately six months (in regions with forty-week seasons). A weekly cash flow report will raise a red flag when it appears that cash flow is not meeting projected budget figures. Cash reserves or a short-term loan will enable a company to meet its financial liabilities. During periods of positive cash flow, excess cash, after expenses, can be invested in short-term securities and investments.

Cash flow reports (Figure 5-4) provide a means of tracking actual income and direct expenses against monthly projections. Since labor is the primary expense of maintenance companies, these reports emphasize projected payroll for the period against projected income. This financial tool is the key that keeps the doors open and the trucks rolling.

financial management
proactive engagement with financial reports, analyzing information, and implementing adjustments to meet budgeted projections.

Financial management is proactive engagement with financial reports, analyzing information, and implementing adjustments wherever necessary to meet budgeted projections. These reviews are of current information on the company's financial status, derived from balance sheets; its profitability status, derived from income statements; and its cash flow status, based on cash flow reports. These three financial entities provide a quantitative analysis of company's current financial status. Monitoring of revenues, costs and expenses, and cash flow keeps managers informed and prepared to meet financial challenges and maintain the company in a profitable mode.

■ Job Cost Management

job cost management
monitoring direct costs, labor and materials, against job budgets.

Profit centers are where the company's financial outcome is determined. An accurate statement in this regard is: "Front line is bottom line." **Job cost management** entails monitoring direct costs, labor and materials, against job budgets. Managers are constantly assessing costs against projected revenue. Each day on the job is equated to work hours with the actual expended time being compared to the budgeted amount of hours (derived from the job estimate). Field reports (Figure 5-5) are generated to provide supervisors with projected hours for the scheduled service or work phase.

	January	February	March
Current Balance			
Cash received			
Sales			
Accounts receivable			
Other			
Total cash received	_____	_____	_____
Cash disbursements			
Fuel			
Insurance			
Interest			
Office expenses			
Inventory—fertilizer			
Inventory—plants			
Payroll			
Payroll taxes			
Professional fees—legal			
Lease—trucks			
Rent			
Utilities			
Other			
Total cash disbursements	_____	_____	_____
Cash Balance	_____	_____	_____

Figure 5-4   Monthly Cash Flow Report

Job # _____
Location _____
Start Date _____
Completion Date _____

Materials	Quantities	Equipment	Hours

Operations/services: Hours

Contact

Contact information:

    Name _____

    Telephone: _____

Figure 5-5   Job Field Report

Weekly summaries indicate which job operations are within budgeted hours and those that are exceeding projections. In instances where labor is over budget, an analysis of the job reports indicates where the overruns are occurring. The job cost management system relies on software programs to produce reports that enable managers to track production costs from start to finish. Knowing the current job status allows for adjustments to be made on a job to put it back on a profitable track.

The information derived from job cost management systems enables companies to bid future work with more accuracy. Labor costs for hardscape installation compared to plant installation can be broken out to determine markups based on productivity levels—in other words, determining the hourly rates or standards based on specific production times. Problems that arise during jobs can be more readily resolved in the future by recognizing a more efficient means of increasing profitability. Examples would be having a chipper available for large pruning jobs, leaf vacuums for leaf removal, or a compact utility loader for a residential installation.

The first layer of a job cost system is the estimate, which projects production hours and costs, material quantities and costs, equipment costs, subcontractors' costs, and other direct costs associated with the job. The costs and quantities are broken out by the service or phase of the job. Once the estimate is accepted, it becomes the budget for the project/job. Each phase/service of the job has cost breakdowns that assist project/account managers in scheduling crews and managing their production hours. Most importantly, the budgeted hours lets field supervisors know how much time they have to get the job done. Labor budgets (Figure 5-6) are set up on a week-to-week basis, and management tracks actual hours to budget. Adjustments are made due to change orders (additional work beyond the contract), weather factors, or any other factors that would cause deviations from the production schedule.

Job cost accountability is achieved through input of daily job reports (Figure 5-7). In Chapter 7 we will see how this task is facilitated by technology such as GPS (global positioning satellite) systems and hand-held PDAs (personal digital assistants). The computerized field reports are uploaded to the company server and directed to payroll and accounting with the job codes and respective production hours. Material entries are also recorded and checked with invoices to ensure that the budget quantities are being directed to the job.

Job/Client Name			Week Ending					
Operation/Service	**Budgeted Hours**	**Actual Hours**	**% Completion**	**M**	**T**	**W**	**Th**	**F**
Total								

Figure 5-6 Weekley Labor Production Sheet

Figure 5-7 Daily Job Report

Another important cost factor is associated with inventory. Each inventory item, whether it is plants, fertilizer, or fieldstone, needs to be accounted for with a job number. Too often inventory items are used on jobs without any record of job allocation. Negligent recording of inventory items prevents recovery of purchase costs and profit and distorts job cost reports (inaccurate material costs). An inventory system assists in tracking where the materials go. Project managers are required to sign for all materials taken from inventory and assign them job numbers. Inventory control is achieved by an inventory manager who is assigned the task of controlling the outflow and maintaining required material quantities.

INVENTORY STOCK LIST

Item Description	Qty. Available	Qty. Min.	Qty. Max.	Qty. on Order

Inventory stock lists provide the current status of materials on hand and the quantities that need to be maintained.
Source: Blueprint for Success, Professional Landcare Network, Herndon, VA, in cooperation with Caterpillar.

purchase order
stipulates the quantity of items ordered and the manger authorizing the purchase.

Materials costs are kept current by posting invoices to jobs as soon as they are received. Receipt of shipments (shipping receipts) is critical to the accuracy of these postings to ensure that the quantities and type of materials correspond to the **purchase orders.**

Job cost reports provide information on actual costs versus budgeted costs:

1. Production hours, current and projected at completion
2. Material costs
3. Projected total cost at completion
4. Total costs in each category

At any given time, a project manger can access the total costs of any one job and compare it to its budget projections. In the example given in Figure 5-8, labor hours are slightly under budget for the month of April and to date for the UMD installation project. Sammy, the project manager, notices that the plant costs are 9% over budget. He checks with the plant purchaser to determine the discrepancy from the budget projection. After checking the plant invoices, they determine that the cost discrepancy is due to a higher unit cost for some 'Bloodgood' London plane trees. This is not uncommon if there is a limited supply of a plant variety or if the item is purchased in small quantities and thus is not eligible for a quantity discount.

In addition to computerized job reports, maintenance companies prefer to have job boards (Figure 5-9) posted that record the weekly status of production hours, actual versus budgeted, for each scheduled service and client property. At a glance, field supervisors can see how much time they have remaining for each job. Adjustments can be made in routing/scheduling jobs to redirect labor hours for completing services that have been delayed, such as mulching when early spring causes mowing to begin earlier. Management might subcontract out to mulching companies that use mulching trucks to complete that phase of the contract.

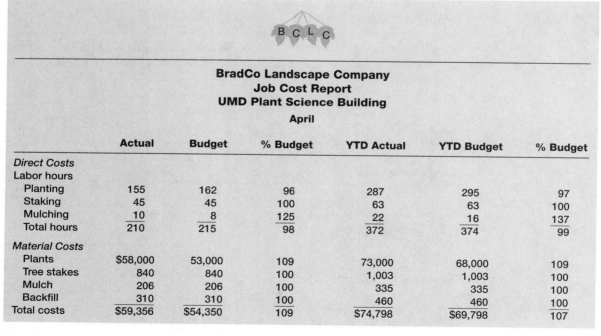

BradCo Landscape Company
Job Cost Report
UMD Plant Science Building
April

	Actual	Budget	% Budget	YTD Actual	YTD Budget	% Budget
Direct Costs						
Labor hours						
Planting	155	162	96	287	295	97
Staking	45	45	100	63	63	100
Mulching	10	8	125	22	16	137
Total hours	210	215	98	372	374	99
Material Costs						
Plants	$58,000	53,000	109	73,000	68,000	109
Tree stakes	840	840	100	1,003	1,003	100
Mulch	206	206	100	335	335	100
Backfill	310	310	100	460	460	100
Total costs	$59,356	$54,350	109	$74,798	$69,798	107

Figure 5-8 Job Cost Report

February							
	Weekly Hours						
Job Site	1	2	3	4	Total Actual	Total Budget	%Budget
Tupper Condos							
Mulching							
Pruning							

Figure 5-9 Monthly Maintenance Service Tracking February

Job budget revisions may be necessary during a job due to weather situations and other unforeseen circumstances, such as delayed delivery of materials. On the other hand, the job may be progressing ahead of schedule due to favorable weather conditions and production efficiency. In both cases, the budget would be revisited and adjustments made in production hours to project the job profit or loss. As previously mentioned, each of these reports becomes a reference document for estimating similar jobs in the future. Collectively, the reports comprise the profit center's income statement that will reflect its profitability.

Landscape construction companies use scheduling boards (Figure 5-10) to post start dates and completion dates. The schedule board may have three to four months of postings. Depending on weather and other factors, the board will be updated with revised start and completion dates. Pertinent information for each job will be listed, such as directions, contact information, job number, location, estimated costs, gross profit, and budgeted direct job costs (materials, labor, subcontracts).

Quarterly and annual job costs reports are issued for each profit center. The costs are compared to the previous year to assess the profit center's profitability. If the bud-

SCEDULE BOARD

Jobs on Schedule						
Jobs to be Scheduled	Monday	Tuesday	Wednesday	Thursday	Friday	Jobs Completed to be Billed

Schedule boards provide a listing of current contracted jobs and date of completion.
Source: Blueprint for Success, Professional Landcare Network, Herndon, VA, in cooperation with Caterpillar.

Job No. _____	Job Client _____		Start Date _____	Completion Date _____

Job No. _____ Job Client _____ Start Date _____ Completion Date _____

Contact _____ Telephone No. _____ Job Location _____

Directions _____

Budgeted Direct Job Costs $_____ Budgeted Gross Profit _____

Materials	Quantity	Unit Cost	Total Cost

Figure 5-10   Schedule Board Job Format

geted profit is not being met, an analysis of costs will indicate where the overage occurs. This cost summary will also indicate whether the productivity level is sufficient and if production standards and pricing need to be adjusted for future jobs.

Tracking direct costs is what job cost management is about. Keeping current with jobs in progress enables management to analyze current information and make adjustments that will increase bottom line profit. In instances where costs exceed budgeted costs in spite of productivity efficiency, there may be a problem with the current estimating process. The objective of job cost management is to monitor and manage. Businesses that succeed in today's competitive market do so by concentrating on improving productivity.

Establishing standards and providing resources such as equipment, training, GPS routing, and so forth leads to greater profitability. Managing operations within each profit center is the key to eliminating waste associated with "call-backs" and downtime. Labor waste is illustrated by Figure 5-11, which demonstrates how daily downtime costs

	15-Minute Loss in Billable Time				
		$ Loss			
No. of Crews*	**Billing Rate/Hour**	**Per Day**	**Per Week**	**Per Month**	**Annually****
1	$35	$8.75	$43.75	$175	$1,837.50
5	$35	$43.75	$218.75	$875	$9,187.50
10	$35	$87.50	$437.50	$1,750	$18,375.00
20	$35	$175.00	$875.00	$3,500	$36,750.00

*Three person
**Based on 42 weeks of production

Per day = .25 × bill rate/hour
Per week = Per day × 5 days
Per month = Per week × 4 weeks
Annually = Per month × 10.5 months

Figure 5-11   Economics of Nonproductive Time

BradCo Landscape Company
College Park Branch
Maintenance Division
October 2004

	Week 1	Week 2	Week 3	Week 4	Total	Budget	% Budget	YTD Total	YTD Budget	YTD %
Direct Hours	12,778	12,788	10,855	11,169	47,590	59,206	80.4	488,684	464,041	105.3
$	112,162	111,724	95,843	98,701	418,429	480,118	87.2	4,241,738	4,087,131	103.8
Indirect Hours	311	152	197	205	864	760	113.6	29,752	22,700	131.10
$	3,085	1,961	2,457	3,064	11,288	8,709	129.6	335,692	287,514	116.80
Overtime $	15,425	15,291	13,934	12,886	57,537	57,863	99.4	577,640	461,240	125.20

Figure 5-12   Tracking Division Job Cost Labor Hours

the company in productive hours and dollars. The time lost may be associated with excessive travel time, fueling, late departure from the yard, breakdown in equipment, or return trips for job equipment or materials.

The loss in billable time is associated with production inefficiency. It's the job of management to determine where the inefficiencies occur and to take corrective actions to eliminate their reccurrence. Regardless of how long a company has been in business, management never becomes complacent about job cost management. There is always room for improvement, and in the competitive environment of the landscape industry, it is essential that a company increase its productivity efficiency to enable it to deliver its services at a profitable and competitive price.

A job cost hours summary sheet enables a quick analysis of labor hours throughout the term of a service contract. It can be cross-referenced to the scheduled services to assess production efficiency. In the report in Figure 5-12, direct hours and dollars expended for labor are fairly close to budgeted figures. However, these differences still raise a red flag and warrant an analysis of the variances. Was it due to weather factors, equipment breakdowns, or errors in estimated budgets? Remember that direct hour costs refers to the labor hours that were applied directly to the job. The indirect hours are 31% over budget, which equates to $48,178 ($335,692 − $287,514). The indirect hours include travel time for trips to the dump, pickup of materials, fueling time, time to load and unload the trucks, and the time it takes the crews to leave the yard. There is obviously waste or downtime, which needs to be identified and rectified. Further exacerbating the labor hours is overtime. Overtime is necessary only when weather conditions, time constraints, or other extenuating circumstances (such as an insufficient labor force) prevail. The overrun in budgeted overtime is $116,400. A control valve for restricting overtime hour overflow is to require account managers to get approval from their branch manager prior to authorizing overtime expenditures.

Total labor cost overruns for the BradCo maintenance division, through October, are $164,732 ($154 direct costs, $48,178 indirect hours, $116,400 overtime). The profit and loss statement for this division at this time would bleed red ink. Questions need to be asked and answers found to enable corrective actions to be taken.

The landscape industry generates revenues through the combined production of equipment and labor. Profit from the generated revenues will be maximized if the amount of production hours for both of the entities is minimized. This can be achieved with a job cost management system.

- Production is the process of performing a task.
- Estimating how long that task will take is also a process.
- Establishing production predictability is the key to recurring profitability.

> ■ "Create constancy of purpose toward improvement of product and service, with the aim to become competitive and to stay in business, and to provide jobs." **W. Edwards Deming** ▮

■ Contract Management

Contract management utilizes job cost management to keep current with daily production costs. It is vital to both maintenance and installation contracts. It is particularly critical for project managers associated with large commercial installation projects. These projects are generally bid on a very competitive basis and therefore are managed on a tight budget with very little room for error. Production inefficiencies, schedule delays, or purchases that exceed budgeted costs all can adversely affect the profitability of the project. Project managers in these situations are responsible for:

- Site management—logistics, scheduling, safety
- Mobilization—equipment, staging holding areas for materials
- Personnel management—scheduling
- Monitoring labor production costs—tracking against budget
- Monitoring purchases—tracking invoices against budget
- Producing invoices—timely issuance
- Monitoring percent of completion—phases of construction
- Recovering retainage (commercial construction)—fulfilling specs on schedule
- Monitoring payables and receivables—tracking
- Warranty management—monitoring and scheduling
- Change order issuance (commercial construction)—additional work
- Inspection for quality control—meeting specifications

work in progress schedule

summarizes current production costs and what has been billed to date.

The project manager will maintain a **work in progress schedule** (WIP) for each project that summarizes the current production costs and what has been billed to date. The daily summary enables the manager to check job hours against budgeted (estimated) hours for every phase of the project. The WIP schedule also reflects the completion stage of the project. This information is vital for maintaining cash flow to meet payables to vendors and subcontractors. General contractors require monthly invoices from the landscape contractor that itemizes what has been completed in the job phase—irrigation, tree installation, sod installation, paver installation, and so on. The landscape company is paid thirty days after the submittal of the invoice.

retainage

the amount of money retained by the general contractor or client, usually 10% of the total contract cost, until all specifications of the contract have been met.

Contracts, particularly commercial contracts, have a **retainage** clause that is generally 10% of the total amount of the contract. This amount is retained by the general contractor/client until the completed landscape installation is inspected and it has been verified that all of the specifications have been met.

Stringent contract management ensures:

- Profit
- Production efficiency
- Production coordination
- Communication with general contractor/client
- Goals will be set and met
- Priorities are set

The mutual goal of job cost management and contract management is to measure where the company is.

> "You are what you measure." **Bruce Hunt, Brickman Group, Ltd.**

Measurement is the key to proactive management and increased profitability.

■ Summary

Financial management involves monitoring the costs of delivering services and implementing corrective actions to maintain profitability. Accounting systems provide the information for management to generate reports and statements that summarize the current financial status of the company, its branches, and individual profit centers.

What are the components of balance sheets and income statements? What are the financial implications of balance sheets and income statements?

Balance sheet components include assets, current and fixed; liabilities, current and long term; and owner's equity. The ratio of assets to liabilities indicates a company's financial stability, reflecting its ability to meet its financial obligations.

Income statements, also referred to as profit and loss statements, consist of a report of current revenues and the direct, indirect costs, and overhead expenses associated with those revenues. The income statement reflects profit or loss for a specific period, based on the difference between costs, expenses, and revenues. Income statements indicate whether a company, its branches, and its profit centers, is operating at a profit.

What are job cost management systems? What is job cost reporting?

Job cost management entails managing day-to-day costs associated with production. Managers compare actual costs of labor and materials against budgets and determine where adjustments need to be made to attain budgeted goals. Job cost estimates serve as the individual job cost budgets. Job cost reports provide the managers with current information regarding actual versus budgeted direct costs. These reports provide actual to budgeted labor hour comparisons, cost of labor, and cost of materials for the respective period, year to date, and percent of the budget.

What are contract management responsibilities?

Contract management responsibilities include site management, mobilization, personal management, generating invoices, monitoring percentage of completion, recovering retainage, warranty management, issuing change orders, and quality control.

■■ Knowledge Application

1. Contrast the differences between balance sheets and income statements in regard to:

   a. Their financial components

   b. Their financial significance

2. Develop a personal cash flow budget that projects your income and expenses over a twelve-month period. You may consider all sources of income including parent subsidies and scholarships.

3. Based on the income statement information for the Terp Landscape Company, what is:

   a. The gross margin for each year?

   b. The net profit for each year?

   c. Your financial assessment of the company?

Terp Landscape Company

	2001	2002	2003
Total sales	$1,520,000	$1,884,800	$2,544,500
Direct costs	819,000	1,005,000	1,323,000
Overhead	581,000	750,000	1,070,000

4. You have just received a weekly job cost report that indicates a $3,000 overrun in labor hours associated with a plant installation project in Washington, D.C.

   a. What factors could possibly contribute to this cost overrun?

   b. What adjustments need to be made to get back on budget?

Financial Ratios

CHAPTER OBJECTIVES

To gain an understanding of:

1. The categories of financial ratios

2. The components of financial ratios

3. How ratios are calculated

4. Ratios as indices of business performance

5. Improving ratios with astute financial management

Ratios provide us with a perspective of relationships between two entities. They are found by dividing the magnitude of one entity into the other. We hear and read about ratios every day, particularly in sports. A college basketball point guard who averages twenty shots per game and makes five baskets has a ratio of baskets/attempted shots of 5/20 or 25%. This information assesses the player's shooting ability, which at 25% would not raise any eyebrows or attract any NBA offers.

Financial ratios also provide an index of performance. They indicate how well a business is financially managed. These ratios are calculated from information extrapolated from financial statements. Business ratios are categorized into liquidity ratios, debt ratios, activity ratios, productivity ratios, and profitability ratios.

■ Liquidity Ratios

liquidity status
a company's ability to pay short-term debts with current assets.

The **liquidity status** of a company indicates its ability to pay short-term debts with current assets. Liquidity refers to the state of being liquid in terms of cash and assets that can be readily converted into cash. Personal liquidity status would include cash in savings and checking accounts, certificates of deposit, and stocks.

liquidity ratios
measure a company's current assets against current liabilities.

Liquidity ratios measure the current assets of a company against its current liabilities. Current assets are those that can be converted into cash within a twelve-month period. These assets include inventory, accounts receivable, cash, and securities, such as certificates of deposit, money market funds, and stocks. *Current liabilities* refer to debts that will be paid within a twelve-month period. These liabilities include loan payments, vendor invoices, state and federal taxes, payroll, insurance premiums, leases, and rent.

Three primary ratios measure a company's ability to meet its current financial obligations with its current assets. These ratios are the current ratio, quick ratio, and cash to current liabilities.

CURRENT RATIO

$$\text{Current ratio} = \frac{\text{Current assets}}{\text{Current liabilities}}$$

Measures ability to pay short-term debt—insurance, vendor invoices, payroll, leases—with cash from savings and checking, accounts, securities, inventory, and accounts receivable

current ratio
indicates a company's ability to meet financial commitments with an available funding resource.

The amount of current assets and current liabilities is obtained from the company's balance sheet. **Current ratio** indicates a company's ability to meet financial commitments with an available funding resource. This is an important index for a company to monitor because of the seasonal fluctuations in the landscape industry. The impact of these fluctuations is evident in the annual cash flow pattern, which inevitably has periods of negative cash flow (expenses exceeding cash income). A ratio of one indicates that for every dollar of liabilities there is a dollar of assets. Therefore, a company with a ratio of one is able to meet its current liabilities or short-term debt with its current assets. Banks and loan institutions refer to the current ratio when reviewing a company's application for a loan or credit line. These institutions prefer a current ratio of two, since it provides a greater safety margin with two dollars of current assets for every dollar of current liabilities.

quick ratio
indicates whether a business is able to pay its short-term debt with cash.

QUICK RATIO

The **quick ratio** is sometimes referred to as the "acid-test ratio" because it indicates whether a business can pay its short-term debt with readily accessible cash. You'll note that the current assets portion of the ratio only includes assets that can be converted into cash in the shortest amount of time. Inventory is not included in the calculation because of the time factor associated with its liquidity. A quick ratio of one is acceptable, indicating that there is $1 of liquid assets available to meet every $1 of current financial obligations.

$$\text{Quick ratio} = \frac{\text{Cash} + \text{Marketable securities} + \text{Accounts receivable}}{\text{Current liabilities}}$$

Measures ability to pay short-term debt with cash from bank accounts, cash from marketable securities, and accounts receivable

CASH TO CURRENT LIABILITIES RATIO

Although companies do not maintain sufficient cash reserves to meet 100% of their liabilities, they do maintain a percentage based on their specific financial needs, for example, payroll, vendor invoices, early payment discounts (usually within ten days of receipt), and loan and lease payments. The **cash to current liabilities ratio** measures a company's ability to meet its financial obligations with actual cash in bank accounts. A general guideline for this ratio would be one.

cash to current liabilities ratio

measures a company's ability to meet its financial obligations with actual cash in bank accounts.

$$\text{Cash to current liabilities} = \frac{\text{Cash}}{\text{Current liabilities}} \times 100$$

Measures ability to pay short-term debt with cash in bank accounts

The primary difference between the liquidity ratios is the source of assets that are used to pay the current debt. The source of assets determines the rapidity with which they can be converted into cash. The assets in the current ratio require the longest time period due to the time required for liquidation of inventory and investments as well as receipt of accounts receivable payments. A portion of the assets in the quick ratio are available immediately from cash in bank accounts and short-term investments such as certificates of deposit, and the remaining assets are available as cash when payments are received from accounts receivable. All of the assets in the cash to current liabilities ratio are immediately available for debt payment, since they are already in cash-based bank balances in checking and savings accounts. The examples that follow will illustrate the significance of these ratios in measuring the company's ability to pay its short-term debts with the various current assets.

The balance sheet that has been created for BradCo Landscape Company (Figure 6-1) will provide the financial information for the ratio calculations, along with information derived from its income statement.

BradCo Landscape Company
Balance Sheet
06/30/04

Assets
  Current assets
    Cash $ 16,300

Assets		
Current assets		
Cash	$ 16,300	
Securities	7,000	
Accounts receivable	132,500	
Inventory	146,800	
Total Current Assets	$302,600	
Fixed Assets		
Buildings/improvements	$360,000	
Equipment and vehicles	158,800	
Furniture and fixtures	50,100	
Depreciation allowance	−25,520	
Total Fixed Assets	$543,380	
Total Assets		$845,980
Liabilities & Owner's Equity		
Current liabilities		
Accounts payable	$ 37,000	
Accrued expenses	27,600	
Taxes payable	3,500	
Notes payable	24,200	
Total Current Liabilities	$ 92,300	
Long-Term Liabilities		
Notes payable	$306,500	
Total Liabilities		$398,800
Owner's equity		
Stock holdings	$212,000	
Retained earnings	235,180	
Total Owner's Equity		$447,180
Total Liabilities and Equity		$845,980

Figure 6-1 A Balance Sheet Summarizes a Company's Assets and Liabilities and Reflects Its Net Worth (Owner's Equity)

BradCo Landscape Company

$$\text{Current ratio} = \frac{\text{Current assets}}{\text{Current liabilities}} = \frac{\$302,600}{\$92,300} = 3.3$$

Industry current ratio averages for the various sectors are:

Design/build   2.2

Exterior maintenance   2.2

Exterior installation   1.9

Source: 2001 Operating Cost Study, Professional Landcare Network and American Nursery and Landscape Assocation, Herndon, VA.

$$\text{Quick ratio} = \frac{\text{Cash} + \text{Accounts receivable}}{\text{Current liabilities}}$$

BradCo Landscape Company

$$\text{Quick ratio} = \frac{\$16,300 + \$132,500}{\$92,300} = \frac{\$148,800}{\$92,300} = 1.6$$

Industry quick ratio averages for the various sectors are:

Design/build   1.8

Exterior maintenance   1.9

Exterior installation   1.4

Source: 2001Operating Cost Study, Professional Landcare Network and American Nursery and Landscape Association, Herndon, VA.

BradCo Landscape Company

$$\text{Cash to current liabilities} = \frac{\text{Cash}}{\text{Current liabilities}} \times 100$$

$$= \frac{\$16,300}{\$92,300} = 0.18 \times 100 = 18\%$$

Industry cash to current liabilities ratio averages for the various sectors are:

Design/build   66.6%

Exterior maintenance   37.9%

Exterior installation   27.1%

So what do these ratios say about the performance of the BradCo Landscape Company? The current ratio indicates that there is $3.30 of current assets for every $1.00 of current liability. Another way of looking at it is that the current assets are 330% of the current liabilities. Regardless of the way it is stated, BradCo Landscape Company has more than sufficient assets that can be converted into cash to meet its twelve-month liabilities.

The quick ratio indicates that there is $1.60 of cash, and accounts receivable assets for every $1 of current liabilities. In other words, the twelve-month liabilities could be paid with the company's cash holdings, securities, and accounts receivable. Keep in mind, however, that the ratio is based on the accounts receivable being current (within thirty to forty days). Therefore, the company's credit department needs to be diligent in managing the accounts receivable to maintain a favorable quick ratio.

The cash to current liabilities ratio shows that there is only $.18 of cash assets for every $1 of short-term debt, or stated in percentage terms, cash assets can meet only 18% of the short-term debt. Cash holdings for the BradCo Landscape Company will be inadequate during periods of negative cash flow and therefore a bigger cash reserve should be maintained to better position the company to be able to meet a larger percentage of its short-term debt. A recommendation would be for the company to reduce its inventory and reallocate the invested dollars into cash accounts or short-term securities. Purchases of inventory in anticipation of allocation to jobs, as in this instance, ties up liquid capital that could be applied to current liabilities.

Taking all of the ratios into consideration, it is evident that current assets in total can meet the company's short-term obligations, but it would require liquidation of most of the current assets. A recommendation for the BradCo Landscape Company would be to build up a larger cash reserve and to be diligent in keeping accounts receivable current.

■ Debt Ratio

debt ratio

measures the amount of a company's debt relative to the owner's equity.

A **debt ratio** measures the amount of a company's debt relative to the owner's equity (amount of money remaining after liabilities are subtracted from assets). It indicates the amount of debt that can be financed by the owner's equity. Companies with ratios larger than one would deter lending institutions from approving a line of credit or loan. Any ratio above one would indicate that the company's debt exceeds the owner's equity.

$$\text{Debt to equity} = \frac{\text{Total liabilities}}{\text{Owner's equity}}$$

BradCo Landscape Company

$$\text{Debt to equity} = \frac{\$398,800}{\$447,180} = .89$$

Industry debt to equity ratio averages are:

Design/build	1.0
Exterior maintenance	1.1
Exterior installation	1.0

Source: 2001Operating Cost Study, Professional Landcare Network and American Nursery and Landscape Association, Herndon, VA.

BradCo's debt ratio of .89 indicates that there is $.89 of debt for every $1 of owner's equity. The company has less debt than equity and is therefore able to fund its business operations without the need for outside financing. Any outside financing will burden the company with additional liabilities associated with the principal and interest of a loan.

■ Activity Ratios

Two business entities that contribute to cash flow are inventory and accounts receivable. Ratios that indicate their activity, conversion into cash, are useful tools for monitoring the period of time it takes for the conversion.

inventory turnover ratio
indicates the frequency with which inventory is converted into cash via sales to jobs.

An **inventory turnover ratio** indicates the frequency with which inventory is converted into cash via sales to jobs. Whether the inventory is fieldstone or maple trees, inventory doesn't provide any sales revenue to the company until it is sold to a job. Management of inventory (inventory control) requires knowledge of the quantity of materials needed and the time frame. Inventory that sits in the yard for long periods costs the company money. In regard to plant materials, there are costs associated with maintenance and losses due to weather factors.

$$\text{Inventory turnover ratio} = \frac{\text{Material costs}}{\text{Average inventory}}$$

BradCo Landscape Company average monthly inventory: $26,845

Material costs: $205,500

$$\text{Inventory turnover ratio} = \frac{\$205,500}{\$26,845} = 7.7$$

BradCo's inventory turnover of 7.7 indicates that its average inventory is converted into cash approximately eight times a year. This turnover rate is less than the industry benchmark for the maintenance sector of the industry. BradCo's management should therefore consider maintaining a smaller inventory of items that can be obtained within a short period of time, such as fertilizers and chemicals.

Inventory average turnover rates for landscape contracting businesses are:

Exterior design/build	4.9
Exterior installation	14.6
Exterior maintenance	11.5

Source: 2001 Operating Cost Study, Professional Landcare Network and American Nursery and Landscape Association, Herndon, VA.

These turnover rates indicate the amount of times the dollar value of the inventory is sold on an annual basis. In order for this ratio to accurately reflect inventory turnover, every item used for a job needs to be assigned a job number. This process ensures that the cost of inventory will be recovered as a direct cost to jobs. Monitoring inventory outflow is an integral part of an inventory control system.

average collection period
the period of time, in days, that it takes a company to collect its accounts receivable.

Accounts receivable has an even more significant impact on cash flow because of the dollars involved. Accounts receivable turnover is expressed as an **average collection period.** This financial indicator reflects the period of time, in days, that it takes a company to collect its accounts receivable.

$$\text{Average collection period} = \frac{365}{\text{Sales/AR}}$$

BradCo Landscape Company

$$\text{Average collection period} = \frac{365}{\$1,370,000/132,500} = \frac{365}{10.3} = 35.4 \text{ days}$$

Since accounts receivable constitute the primary cash flow entity of landscape companies, their accounting departments need to be diligent in invoicing and collecting payments. BradCo's average collection period falls within the good range of thirty to forty days.

Average collection days for various sectors of the landscape industry are:

Exterior design/build   32.6

Exterior installation   45.3

Exterior maintenance   36.2

Source: 2001 Operating Cost Study, Professional Landcare Network and American Nursery and Landscape Association, Herndon, VA.

Another business activity that warrants close monitoring is accounts payable. The period of time it takes a company to pay its vendors (suppliers) is indicative of a company's financial management. Vendors will check a company's **accounts payable payout period** prior to extending credit. This information can be derived from business subscription services such as Dun and Bradstreet.

accounts payable payout period

indicates the time a company takes to pay its vendors.

The number of days a company takes to pay its vendors is calculated by the formula:

$$\text{Accounts payable payout period} = \frac{\text{Accounts payable}}{\text{Cost of goods sold/365 days}}$$

BradCo Landscape Company

$$\text{Accounts payable period} = \frac{\$37,000}{\$205,500/365} = \frac{\$37,000}{563} = 66 \text{ days}$$

Industry average days for accounts payable period for the various sectors:

Exterior design/build   32.6

Exterior installation   45.4

Exterior maintenance   36.2

Source: 2001 Operating Cost Study, Professional Landcare Network and American Nursery and Landscape Association, Herndon, VA.

Vendors will grant credit without reservation to companies that pay their invoices within thirty to forty days. If the timeliness of payments exceeds sixty days, vendors may require C.O.D. (cash on delivery) for materials/supplies. In the BradCo Landscape Company example, all of their vendors will require C.O.D. on all orders until delinquent invoices are paid. These delinquent invoices may be associated with inadequate cash reserves due to excessive inventory, delinquent accounts receivable, and/or negative cash flow associated with a large installation project(s). A new company normally will have to do business with a vendor for several months to a year to establish an acceptable payable period (thirty to forty days) before credit will be extended.

BradCo Landscape Company
Income Statement
6/30/05

Net Sales	$1,370,000
Direct Costs	
Labor	383,600
Materials	205,500
Subcontractors	82,200
Total Direct Costs	$ 671,300
Gross Margin	$ 698,700
Indirect Overhead	$ 191,800
G & A Overhead	$ 356,200
Pretax Profit	$ 150,700

Figure 6-2 A Company's Income Statement Indicates the Current Profitability of Its Operations For the Respective Statement Period

The above income statement (Figure 6-2), along with the previous balance statement, provide financial information for the productivity and profitability calculations that follow.

■ Productivity Ratios

Two primary ratios reflect the productivity of a company. One relates to employees, and the other relates to fixed assets. They are both indicators of the efficient use of these production resources.

LABOR COSTS

Labor is the largest cost category on a landscape company's income statement. It is the goal of every company to maximize the production from its labor force. As productivity increases, the return on labor costs will be reflected in the ratio of sales per employee.

$$\text{Sales per employee} = \frac{\text{Net sales}}{\text{Full-time equivalent employees}}$$

BradCo Landscape Company

$$\text{Sales per employee} = \frac{\$1,370,000}{25} = \$54,800$$

The employee sales ratio of $54,800 is indicative of the amount of production dollars that can be generated by BradCo Landscapes full-time profit center employees. Seasonal employees are also allocated into the full-time equivalents. They are accounted for on the basis of two seasonal employees being equivalent to one full-time employee.

In addition to indicating the sales dollars of FTEs, this ratio also assists the company in planning for growth. Based on the sales productivity of employees, management can project the number of employees needed to meet a projected sales figure. If the sales productivity per employee is not being maintained annually, technical training, employee motivation, and equipment assessment may be required. Although the benchmarks below reflect industry averages, the benchmarks within a company are management's benchmarks. By analyzing company and division productivity ratios, management can identify which factors will increase production efficiency, such as equipment, scheduling, or training.

Industry averages for sales per employee among the various sectors are:

Exterior design/build $80,989

Exterior installation $77,926

Exterior maintenance $62,370

Source: 2001 Operating Cost Study, Professional Landcare Network and American Nursery and Landscape Association, Herndon, VA.

FIXED ASSETS

Equipment is the largest component of a landscape company's fixed assets. The return on this capital investment is based on the amount of production (sales) that it generates. The productivity ratio for fixed assets is found with the following calculation:

$$\text{Sales to fixed assets} = \frac{\text{Net sales}}{\text{Fixed assets}}$$

BradCo Landscape Company

$$\text{Sales to fixed assets} = \frac{\$1,370,000}{\$543,380} = 2.5$$

The 2.5 ratio in the example indicates that for every $1 of BradCo Landscape Company's fixed assets, $2.50 in sales is generated. The significance of the ratio is that it manifests the utilization of fixed assets. Sales to fixed assets actually represents the percentage of return from the invested dollars in fixed assets. Since equipment and vehicles are major components of these assets, the ratio indicates their employment in sales production. In this example, BradCo Landscape Company's low ratio reflects an investment in buildings and improvements for a new branch location ($360,000). As additional sales are generated from this branch, the percentage return from fixed assets will increase.

Industry averages for sales to fixed assets among the various sectors are:

Exterior design/build   8.4%

Exterior installation   9.7%

Exterior maintenance   8.3 %

Source: 2001 Operating Cost Study, Professional Landcare Network and American Nursery and Landscape Association, Herndon, VA.

■■ Profitability Ratios

profitability

measured in relation to sales, total assets, and net worth.

gross margin

measures profitability after direct costs associated with production are subtracted from sales.

Additional indices of a company's financial performance are profitability ratios. The **profitability** of a company is measured in relation to sales, total assets, and net worth.

Gross margin measures profitability after direct costs associated with production are subtracted from sales.

$$\text{Gross margin} = \frac{\text{Gross profit dollars}}{\text{Net sales}} \times 100$$

BradCo Landscape Company

$$\text{Gross margin} = \frac{\$698,700}{\$1,370,000} \times 100 = 51\%$$

The average gross margin percentage for the various industry sectors is:

Exterior design/build   43.6%

Exterior installation   39.0%

Exterior maintenance   46.9%

Gross margins are an indication of cost management. The more efficient a company is in its production of services, the larger the gross margin will be as a result of reduced costs. Based on financial history, the gross margin benchmark must be met to attain projected net profits, assuming overhead and administrative expenses remain relatively constant.

profit margin

measures the percentage of profit after direct costs and overhead are subtracted from sales.

Profit margin measures the percentage of profit after direct costs and overhead are subtracted from sales. It provides another index with which companies can assess their financial performance against competitors. Trade association surveys provide benchmarks that are representative of specific sectors within the landscape industry.

$$\text{Profit margin} = \frac{\text{Profit before taxes}}{\text{Net sales}} \times 100$$

BradCo Landscape Company

$$\text{Profit margin} = \frac{\$150,700}{\$1,370,000} \times 100 = 11\%$$

The average profit margin percentage for the industry sectors are:

Exterior design/build	4.3% average
	16.0% high-profit companies
Exterior installation	3.8% average
	9.7% high-profit companies
Exterior maintenance	4.6% average
	12.0% high-profit companies

The bottom line is profit, which is the primary indicator of a company's production efficiency. Production efficiency is the primary factor associated with high-profit companies. Profit is the fuel for the company's growth engines; the larger the fuel supply, the faster the engines will drive the company ahead of its competition. BradCo's 11% net profit indicates both production efficiency and astute overhead cost management.

return on assets (ROA)
indicates the amount of profit generated by the company's total assets.

return on net worth
measures the percentage of profit based on the company's net worth.

Two additional measures of profitability are **return on assets (ROA)** and **return on net worth** (owner's equity). These two ratios are of particular interest to owners and stockholders. They both reflect the return on dollars that are invested into the business.

The return on assets measures the profit as a percentage of the company's assets.

$$\text{Return on assets} = \frac{\text{Profit before taxes}}{\text{Total assets}} \times 100$$

BradCo Landscape Company
$$\text{Return on assets} = \frac{\$150,700}{\$845,980} \times 100 = 18\%$$

The BradCo Landscape Company's ROA indicates that for every dollar it has invested in total assets (current and fixed) it receives a return of $.18 or 18%. The profitability of the remainder of the year will determine whether this percentage of return prevails. Contributing to this rate of return is management of production costs and capital investments in equipment. In regard to the latter, BradCo rents most of the large equipment required for its installation projects.

The industry averages for return on assets are:

Exterior design/build	14.2%
Exterior installation	12.4%
Exterior maintenance	16.3%

Source: 2001 Operating Cost Study, Professional Landcare Network and American Nursery and Landscape Association, Herndon, VA.

The ROA indicates the amount of profit that is being generated by the company's total assets. The exterior maintenance contractor ROA average of 16.3% indicates that the average return for those companies is $.16 for every $1 of company assets. A business owner would be satisfied with any percentage that exceeds what the same asset dollars could return in banks or securities.

The return on net worth measures the percentage of profit based on the company's net worth.

$$\text{Return on net worth} = \frac{\text{Profit before taxes}}{\text{Net worth}} \times 100$$

It may also be expressed as

$$\text{Return on equity} = \frac{\text{Profit before taxes}}{\text{Owner's equity}} \times 100$$

BradCo Landscape Company

$$\text{Return on equity} = \frac{\$150,700}{\$447,180} \times 100 = 33.7\%$$

The owners of the BradCo Landscape Company are receiving 33.7% return from their equity holdings in the company. This is a very good return in contrast to alternative investment options. In addition, this return is a positive reflection of management's ability to control costs and thereby produce a favorable level of profitability.

Industry sector averages for return on net worth/owner's equity are:

Design/build	32.0
Exterior maintenance	32.3
Exterior installation	26.1

The terms *company's net worth* and *owner's equity* are synonymous in that they both represent the amount of money invested in the company after all liabilities have been met. Think of it in the same way as equity that remains in a house. That equity represents the amount of money invested in the house that is the difference between the mortgage balance (liability) and the value of the house (total revenues). The return on owner's equity/company net worth indicates what these invested dollars are earning based on the profitability of the company. Regardless of a favorable ROA, this does not merit complacency, since the management of assets, such as accounts receivable, can always be improved and thereby increase the percentage of return on equity.

The return on assets and return on net worth/owner's equity ratios are measures of performance in relation to investment. The former reflects the return on asset investment and the latter reflects the return on every dollar invested by the owners. Both of the investment returns ratios are affected by two profitability ratios, gross margin and profit margin. Each of these ratios represents opportunities through astute financial management to increase the return on a company's investment. The gross margin is the end result of direct cost management, and profit margin is the end result of total cost and expense management, direct, indirect, and overhead.

Although additional ratios are used by financial analysts to assess company performance, those discussed in this chapter represent the primary financial assessment ratios. The ratios are additional tools for the financial toolbox. They assist management in measuring where the company is in relation to industry benchmarks and the company's financial history.

> "Financial analysis begins where accounting statements end." **Understanding Business 4th edition, William Nickels, James McHugh, Susan McHugh.**

■ Summary

Financial ratios are measurement tools. They provide a means of assessing the company's financial strengths and weaknesses as well as the performance of management.

What are the categories and components of financial ratios?

- Liquidity ratios measure the assets of a company against its liabilities. They indicate a company's ability to meet financial obligations with its assets. The ratios include the current ratio, quick ratio, and cash to current ratio. The computation of these ratios varies based on the liquidity of the assets used in their calculation.

- The debt ratio measures a company's debt relative to owner's equity. It provides an index of the amount of debt that can be financed by the owner's equity.

- Activity ratios measure the period of time required to convert inventory and accounts receivable into cash. Inventory turnover measures the frequency with which the total dollar inventory value is converted into cash as sales to jobs. The average collection period measures the average amount of days required to collect accounts receivable. The accounts payable period measures the amount of days a company takes to pay its suppliers.

- Productivity ratios measure the production of personnel and assets. Sales per employee are an index of individual productivity based on dollars of sale produced in relation to the number of full-time employees. Sales to fixed assets measures the amount of production that is the result of fixed asset allocation. It is an index of how effectively fixed assets are utilized.

- Profitability ratios measure the profitability of sales and invested dollars from assets and owner's equity (net worth). Gross margin is an index of the profit generated after direct costs have been deducted from sales. Profit margin measures the profitability of sales income after direct costs and overhead costs have been deducted. Return on assets reflects the profit generated by the company's total assets. Return on equity indicates the profit produced from an owner's invested dollars.

Why are financial ratios indices of business performance?

Each of these ratios measure the company's performance and also serve as a report card of how well management is doing.

How can management improve the ratios?

Employing these financial tools provides management an opportunity to fix and adjust factors that will improve production efficiency and profitability.

■■ Knowledge Application

1. Calculate the following ratios from the financial data provided:

Todd & Son Landscape Company

Total sales	$2,544,500
Cash	61,000
Inventory	185,000
Securities	6,000
Accounts receivable	269,000
Current liabilities	375,300
Total liabilities	619,900
Net worth	409,700
Cost of goods sold	205,500

    a. Current ratio

    b. Quick ratio

    c. Debt to equity

    d. Accounts payable payout period

2. What is your financial assessment of the calculated ratios in reference to:

    a. The ability of the company to meet its financial obligations?

    b. The company's ability to pay its debt with its net worth?

    c. Timeliness in accounts receivable collections?

3. What would be your goal for inventory turnover? How would you manage inventory to achieve this goal?

4. The management of Todd & Son Landscape Company has increased its gross margin from 35% to 45%, but its net profit remains at 4%.

    a. What can be attributed to the increase in gross margin?

    b. Why hasn't net profit increased with the increased gross margin?

CHAPTER 7

Software Applications

CHAPTER OBJECTIVES

To gain an understanding of:

1. Software system applications for the landscape industry

2. System integration of business management modules

3. Software system applications in the field

Computer technology has revolutionized the business world. Technology that initially facilitated data processing and record storage is now employed to service customers and provide integrated business management systems. Think of how often your daily life interfaces with computers just from the standpoint of meeting your consumer needs. Electronic banking lets you pay your bills; a stop at the automated teller gives you 24/7 access to cash; avoiding long lines, you step up to the computerized ticketing machines at the airport or movie theater; running into the grocery store for a few items, you check out in the self-service aisle where an automated system scans your items and even talks you through the process. When it's time to register for next semester's classes, you're able to complete the process at your computer. In addition to delivery of services, e-business enables us to shop for cars, gifts, vacations, mortgages, and every other conceivable commodity.

Efficient and expedient technology has changed the way we conduct our personal business and the way businesses market and sell their products and services. Businesses have substantially lowered their overhead by reducing the number of personnel required to generate and process sales. The technology has also enabled permanent records to be established for each transaction, reflecting the purchasing patterns and demographics of the customer base. Although landscape companies can't deliver their services with computer technology, they can benefit from the expediency and efficiency associated with computerized information processing. Its implementation has enabled companies to increase their productivity and their ability to access their current financial status.

There are numerous software programs that have applications for the landscape industry. These programs are used to aid in:

- Accounting
- Budgeting
- Estimating
- Job cost management
- Contract management
- Scheduling and routing
- Remote data collection
- Mobile resource management
- Design development
- Irrigation management
- Sales management

Management decisions regarding IT (information technology) implementation revolve around what information needs to be accessed on a daily basis. Current access to job cost management information enables detection of production inefficiencies. Analysis of actual versus budgeted costs reveals production overages and enables adjustments to be made prior to job completion. Management needs to know the daily financial status of the company, its branches and divisions. "With passion we strive to understand and measure where we are," declared Bruce Hunt, vice president of the Brickman Group, Ltd., in relating his company's philosophy. He further stated that corporations who do not abide by this philosophy will encounter financial failures.

"With passion we strive to understand and measure where we are."   **Bruce Hunt**

Knowing where you are enables you to make adjustments that will redirect you to where you want to be. These adjustments cannot be made without historical information derived from current financial reports.

Information technology provides the infrastructure for information management systems. The management aspect pertains to categorizing and interfacing information that is subsequently incorporated into report formats.

Of the many software accounting/management systems available on today's market, the decision on which program(s) to implement in a company should be made by the accountant and the users: executives, managers, accounting staff, and other individuals such as estimators who input or access data. Some of the criteria that may be used to assist in the selection include:

1. Linkage between accounting operations
2. Industry database
3. Current and future needs
4. Availability of technical support
5. User friendliness
6. Report capabilities

Examples of information management systems available to the landscape contracting industry are presented in the following discussion.

■■ Accounting Systems

This is the starting point for developing an integrated management system. The use of accounting software provides expediency and efficiency in integrating financial information for generating financial reports. The database in this system is the hub from which management extrapolates financial information for its day-to-day decisions. Budgets are updated on the foundation of current financial information, such as contract sales and job backlogs. Account managers are able to monitor their accounts' status by comparing the actual versus budgeted production hours and making adjustments. Branch managers are able to track each account manager's accounts and raise a red flag when necessary. Income statements reflect whether the company and individual divisions are meeting their projected profit margins.

Companies need to adapt existing programs to their accounting system. It may take a year working with consultants or technical support before the system works to the satisfaction of the accounting department and management personnel. Some companies opt to retain consultants to customize their own program. Regardless of its origin, the common denominator for all accounting systems should be integration. The value of an integrated accounting system is its ability to interface with estimating, budgeting, and job cost management.

> ■ The value of an integrated accounting system is its ability to interface with estimating, budgeting, and job cost management. ■

Users must be able to extrapolate data such as production rates from the system and integrate the data into desired formats, such as job estimates.

The software should also have the versatility to interface with external hardware, accepting estimating and job cost information from personal digital assistants (PDAs), time card entry systems, fuel pump systems that track individual vehicle consumption, and GPS (global position satellite) tracking systems and routing programs.

■ Web Access

Companies with multiple branches prefer to have one server that can accommodate all branches (rather than separate servers). This can be accomplished through Web access with security codes issued for various levels of managers. District and regional managers utilize these systems to keep current with each branch. Groundskeeper, based in Tucson, Arizona, has six branches in two states and more than 500 employees. It now handles all of its accounts with one integrated system rather than treating the branches as six different companies. Implementing this system has resulted in a 40% reduction in the accounting staff. The system has also improved the generation of custom financial reports. The customized programming feature enables Groundskeeper's accounting department to generate payroll edit reports that can be run for every employee, region, branch, or department. These reports can be generated at any time, thereby improving management's ability to track labor hours. Since the system is user friendly, managers in all branches are assigned user account access through the company network, which lets managers generate weekly or daily profit and loss statements, as well as other reports.

TruGreen LandCare, a division of ServiceMaster, Memphis, Tennessee, also employs a Web-based management system to access current financial information from its regional branches. Regional offices post their budgets, sales, and financial statements online, enabling comparisons of sales and profits to be made regionally and nationally. Web access for this national corporation has had a significant impact on reducing capital expenditures and the overhead associated with servers. Branch offices are able to transmit their data directly to corporate offices through their PCs. Security codes limit access based on the management level of personnel. Branch and regional managers have broader access to financial databases than do account managers. Corporate databases also enable branches to access equipment specifications, pricing and purchasing online.

■ Reporting Systems

All accounting software interfaces with a reporting tool/system. There are several programs available for creating reports. Some of these programs have the capability of creating reports from any type of database and integrating them with Web and Windows® applications. The reports can be formatted to print on preprinted forms or with customized fields and alignments.

Reporting programs format accounting information to assist management with day-to-day operations. They enable management to generate reports for any desired financial analysis, for example, job cost breakdown by service lines, maintenance, installation, job cost analyses on a daily or weekly basis, monthly income statements, job proposals, estimates, or profit center budget versus actual comparisons.

■ Sales Reports

Weekly update reports of sales booked versus sales goals are an important barometer for all sectors of the landscape industry. Sales reports are broken down into contract renewals, pending, and hot leads with probability. This information is posted in weekly reports to provide current tracking and direction for the sales staff.

Each region of the country, based on its weather pattern, has a certain number of weeks during which landscape jobs can be scheduled. Therefore, regional and branch managers need to monitor the amount of business that is being contracted to stay on track for budgeted revenue goals. In the mid-Atlantic region, for example, jobs generally can be scheduled over a forty-two-week period. Maintenance companies in this region of the country strive to have 80–90% of their annual contracts by mid-April.

■ Estimating

Estimating software interfaces with databases of production standards, labor rates, material costs, overhead markups, and profit margins, for example, to generate job estimates.

■ Estimating software interfaces with databases to generate job estimates. ■

Some programs enable digital square footage take-offs (using a computer-linked digitizer) from blueprints or plat plans to be incorporated directly into a spreadsheet. Input of this information enables the system to estimate plant number requirements based on plant spacing specifications as well as hardscape materials.

Once the estimate is finalized, it can be formatted into a job cost budget that allocates direct costs over the duration of the contract. Field reports also can be generated on a daily or weekly basis to provide supervisors with labor and material allocations.

Interfacing the estimating system with the reporting system enables tracking of the job cost status and its projected cost at completion.

■ Interfacing the estimating system with the reporting system enables tracking of job cost status. ■

Reports that further assist job cost management provide pertinent information on material purchasing (procurement), summarizing actual versus budgeted material costs, and project contract history, documenting past transactions and current status.

An additional feature offered by some project management programs is bar coding. Bar coding systems are used for work orders, enabling scanning into the production database without the need of manual data entry. Invoices and statements also can be bar coded and scanned directly into the client's file.

■ Personal Digital Assistants

The hand-held computerized devices known as personal digital assistants (PDAs) have become an asset to the landscape industry. They save time and provide a means of accurately reporting production hours for job cost tracking. Start and stop entries at job sites provide an accurate record of job cost hours. Scheduling is one of the most effective uses of PDAs. Field supervisors can download their next day's schedule from their own PCs at home or from the branch office. Estimating also can be done with a PDA, which expedites site estimating and enables the data to be interfaced with an accounting system. These mobile devices, in tandem with portable printers, also can be used to generate invoices on job sites.

PDA Functions

- Start and stop job times
- Material cost tracking
- Inventory updates
- Scheduling
- Accessing customer files

Yardmaster, Inc. of Painesville, Ohio equips their crews with Palm Pilots®. When they arrive at a job site, the crews select the client from a list stored on the PDA. They then select the service to be performed and the estimated work hours. When the service is completed, they select the next service or property. The Palm Pilot® software has a built-in clock that enables recording of start and stop times for the entire crew along with the completed services. At the end of the day, the units are turned in to the supervisor for downloading. The entire day's jobs have been recorded without the need of any paperwork. The supervisor downloads the information into a PC and immediately is able to compare actual hours to estimated hours while transferring the data to payroll and job costing.

Payroll, job costing, estimating, billing, and scheduling are integrated into PDA software. The scheduling function extrapolates data from the estimating database, which prevents work being done on a job that wasn't in the estimate. If one property has two prunings scheduled while another has only one, the foreman will reference this information from the PDA. As a result of the scheduling function, extra nonbillable services are less likely to occur, and services sold are less likely to be forgotten. Yardmaster is able to load and download their Palm Pilots® at branch offices by accessing their network over the Internet.

Irrigation contractors can utilize Rain Bird Pro® on their PDAs. The features of this software program include scheduling crews, billing, and inventory control. The latter is accomplished by the field supervisor who enters the parts used on the job, which then are deducted from the inventory maintained on the truck. As with other programs specific information on installation and maintenance are easily accessed from the PDA database.

■ Design Software

There are numerous computerized landscape design programs, some of which are AutoCAD-based. As with other software programs, the company's application needs determine program selection. The new generation of design programs is multidimensional and provides realistic perspectives of landscape features. Some of the features that have been integrated into these programs include:

- AutoCAD integration
- Property surveys, plats, etc.
- Preset symbols, layers, and modes
- 3-D imaging for terrain models
- 3-D freeform modeling
- Mass modeling tool that enables building representation in urban settings
- 2-D graphics for drafting
- Outputs with hand-drawn appearance creating drawing sheets with links to elevation and perspective views
- Labeling
- Web-based plan search
- Automated material take-offs
- Links to quotations
- Built-in database and spreadsheet capabilities for generating estimating reports with links to drawings to update reports and schedules
- Grading plan features
- Shadow studies and solar animations
- Plant databases
- Depiction of plant styles
- Night lighting data
- Irrigation components and spray patterns
- Plant placement
- Hardscape materials
- Plan issuance records
- High-end presentations with renderings and animated movies
- Team designing and editing feature

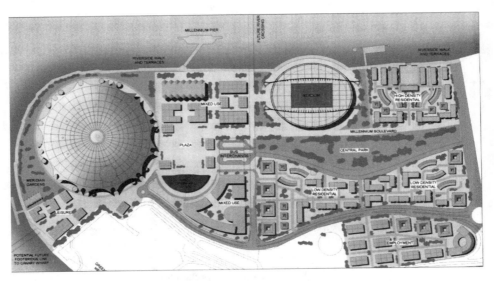

The Above Illustration Is an Example of the Versatility of an Imaging Program—In Essence, This Image Is a Digitized Rendering

On a more simplified scale, landscape concepts and presentations can be generated with digital imaging systems. These systems enable incorporating a footprint of the existing site, such as an entry drive with desired features, from the program's database, such as paver patterns. These databases may be expanded with the user's images.

■ Routing and Tracking

As landscape companies expand their geographic service area, tracking and routing becomes cumbersome. Through the use of innovative technology, this task has been transformed into an efficient and accurate computerized information system, thanks to the U.S. government, which has made its global positioning system (GPS) available for civilian use. GPS was developed for defensive purposes and is funded and operated by the U.S. military. Through this system, coded satellite signals are transmitted and processed by GPS receivers. The receivers translate the signals into position, velocity, and time.

The integration of GPS technology and mapping software has enabled companies to maximize crew efficiency through routing and scheduling of clients.

> ■ The integration of GPS technology and mapping software has enabled companies to maximize crew efficiency through routing and scheduling of clients. ■

Downtime is reduced by utilizing the most direct routes, particularly during periods of construction, and by scheduling clients in close proximity to one another. Additional software features provide Web access, which enables managers and supervisors to communicate.

Managers can track how long a crew has been spending on a job site as well as the location of vehicles and their travel times. Reports can be generated at the end of the day by downloading GPS units manually into PCs or automatically via receiver units. Reports are generated from these programs that document hours spent at specific job sites for each employee, travel time, travel speeds, and hours in service.

■ Mobile Resource Management Systems

The integration of GPS technology with business management systems is referred to as mobile resource management systems (MRM). Most of these systems use wireless communication with cell phones and text messaging, transmitting data collected by GPS units. This Web access enables branch offices to print out their reports through one centralized server. The MRM system provides managers the opportunity to view a job in progress and to assess productivity based on the budgeted labor hours. This information technology system is an excellent example of real-time management.

Routing software has the capability of reorganizing routes in minutes in the event of client cancellations or other factors arising, such as weather or hazardous situations. This information can be transmitted directly to supervisors in the field. Managers can actually transmit messages and rescheduling updates instantaneously from their office PC. The program also offers the opportunity to generate reports, designating all jobs that are currently in progress within a specific radius. This feature enables routing in a logical sequence, thereby reducing travel time. This is another example of real-time management and maximizing production efficiency.

Computer technology is an integral part of business management. It mechanizes data processing and provides instant visualization via reporting formats. This technological resource enables management to be proactive in making adjustments that will improve bottom line profit.

■ Summary

Virtually every aspect of business management can be accommodated efficiently and effectively with computer software. Accounting systems are the most important of the computing tools, with mobile data processing and GPS tracking systems following in importance. The reason for investing in computer technology is the benefits a company will derive from it and how it will affect the bottom line.

What are some software applications for the landscape industry?

Accounting—Monitor company profitability in branches and profit centers

Budget management—Track actual versus budgeted projections

Job cost management—Track job production costs

Estimating—Generate estimates, job budgets, field reports

Collection management—Track accounts receivable

Mobile resource management—Routing, scheduling, job cost management

Design—Plan development and client presentations

How are business management modules integrated through software programs?

Software programs are icons of production efficiency. They expedite data entry and financial reporting, which enables management to analyze and implement production efficiency measures. They provide real-time financial data that enables management to be proactive in budget management. Programs adapted to PDAs also enhance the accuracy and processing of job cost data, scheduling updates, work orders, invoicing, estimating, and inventory management.

Tracking is a keyboard away with the development of real-time monitoring via GPS units, which incorporate software for data entry and transmission via the Internet. Managers can be at their office PCs while tracking jobs in progress and identifying areas for adjustments. Systems that incorporate real-time tracking are referred to as mobile resource management systems.

■ Knowledge Application

1. Based on your daily encounters with business entities, identify where information technology could be implemented to enhance production (transaction) efficiency.

2. Incorporate three landscape software applications from the list in the text into landscape business operations. Discuss their implementation and how they would increase production efficiency.

3. Describe how Web access can be used to communicate with a landscape company's client base.

4. List and describe three applications of mobile resource management to design/build companies.

Managing Human Assets

8

CHAPTER OBJECTIVES

To gain an understanding of:

1. Establishing employee identity
2. Job description components
3. The recruiting process
4. Hiring legalities
5. Creating a company culture
6. Retaining employees
7. Terminating employees

Americans with
    Disabilities
    Act (ADA)
internship programs
interview process

The perspective of viewing employees as company assets is clearly stated in the following quotes.

> "A great deal of the value of a company lies between the ears of its employees." **Marcus Buckingham & Curt Coffman**
> *First, Break All the Rules*

> "Front line is bottom line." **The Disney Keys to Success**

> "Every day 95% of my assets leave through the gates of this company. It is my job to see that they come back." **President, SAS**

Landscape companies that have experienced growth and profitability can attest to the validity of these statements. Whether it is a design/build, construction, or a maintenance business, management is cognizant of the fact that it isn't the equipment that returns dividends, it is the person operating the equipment.

The manner in which the human assets are managed is a determining factor in the growth and profitability of a company.

> How human assets are managed impacts the growth and profitability of a company. ▮

Unlike capital assets, which can be depreciated and readily replaced, personnel assets must be appreciated and are not easily replaced, particularly in the landscape industry. Furthermore, when a human asset leaves a company, his or her value often is transferred to a competitor. Retention of these assets is contingent upon company culture, a topic that is discussed in the latter part of this chapter.

An integral part of a company's culture is the recognition of employees as links in its chain to success. Identifying these links in job descriptions enables these individuals to know what their responsibilities are and what their role is within the company.

■■ Job Descriptions

The job description provides an identity for employees and clearly defines their responsibilities and functions in their positions. It also provides employees and supervisors with indices of job performance and salaries. The description encompasses the qualifications required for the specific job title. Examples of qualifications for landscape industry positions would include the following:

- Physical abilities, such as lifting requirements
- Supervisory skills
- Equipment operation abilities
- License/certification requirements
- Multilingual communication skills, such as Spanish and English
- Sales experience
- Design skills
- Business management experience
- Estimating and bidding experience
- Bachelor's or associate's degree in horticulture or landscape contracting

The primary components of a job description are listed in Figure 8-1. See Figure 8-2 for an example of a landscape company job description.

Americans with Disabilities Act
federal regulations pertaining to compliance with physical, mental, and emotional job requirements.

Item 4 refers to functions that are essential to the job and that cannot be reassigned to another position, eliminated, or accommodated with additional or artificial aid. The basis for this descriptive listing is to comply with regulations of the **Americans with Disabilities Act (ADA).** These federal regulations specifically address physical, mental, and emotional job requirements. In the landscape industry, operating

1. Title—specifically related to the responsibilities of the job
2. Summary—a concise summation of the job in terms of its functional role in the company
3. Accountabilities—a list of expected results for management and tasks for nonmanagement personnel
4. Physical requirements—as they relate to compliance with the Americans with Disabilities Act (ADA) and other physical criteria
5. Working conditions—the physical working environment as it pertains to field and office personnel, such as multitasking, weather elements, noise, fast-paced, team-oriented, overtime, and weekends
6. Supervisory responsibilities—job titles responsible for supervising

Figure 8-1 Job Description Components

Landscape Maintenance Company

Job Title: Area Manager
Department: Commercial Maintenance
Reports To: Division Manager
Prepared Date: March 25, 2006
Approved By: David Thomas
Approved Date: March 30, 2006

Summary
The primary purpose of this job is to oversee a group of crews and provide support and coordination for assigned crew supervisors. Ultimate responsibility: ensuring budgeted and quality performance of assigned projects.

Essential Duties and Responsibilities include the following. Other duties may be assigned.
1. Adhere to company policies.
2. Maintain a professional appearance and attitude.
3. Desire to increase industry knowledge and its application.
4. Desire to grow and advance with the company.
5. Perform required duties in an efficient and quality-oriented manner. Duties include various labor-oriented tasks in our various profit centers.
6. Review and grade subordinate employees on a monthly basis.
7. Recruit employees.
8. Be involved with marketing and sales.
9. Train assigned crew supervisors.
10. Deal with personnel issues.
11. Be involved in success and growth of the company as a top priority.
12. Assist in snow removal.

Supervisory Responsibilities
Manages 1–5 subordinate supervisors who supervise a total of 6–20 employees in their landscape crews. Responsible for overall direction, coordination, and evaluation of unit. Carries out supervisory responsibilities in accordance with the company's policies and applicable laws. Responsibilities include interviewing, hiring, and training employees; planning, assigning, and directing work; appraising performance; rewarding and disciplining employees; addressing complaints and resolving problems.

Qualifications
To perform this job successfully, an individual must be able to perform each essential duty satisfactorily. The requirements listed below are representative of the knowledge, skill, and ability required for such performance. Reasonable accommodations may be made to enable individuals with disabilities to perform the essential functions.

Figure 8-2 Sample Job Description

Education/Experience

Bachelor of Science or Bachelor of Arts degree (B.S. or B.A.) from a four-year college or university; two years related experience or training, or an equivalent combination of education and experience.

Language Skills

Ability to read, analyze, and interpret general business periodicals, professional journals, technical procedures, or governmental regulations. Ability to write reports, business correspondence, and procedure manuals. Ability to effectively present information and respond to questions from groups of managers, clients, and the general public. Ability to converse in Spanish.

Mathematical Skills

Ability to calculate figures and amounts, e.g., discounts, interest, commissions, proportions, percentages, area, circumference, and volume. Ability to apply concepts of basic algebra and geometry.

Reasoning Ability

Ability to define problems, collect data, establish facts, and draw valid conclusions. Ability to interpret an extensive variety of technical instructions in mathematical or diagram form and deal with several abstract and concrete variables. Ability to interpret financial reports and utilize the information for profit enhancement.

Certificates, Licenses, Registrations

Valid Maryland driver's license. Registration with the Maryland Department of Agriculture for application of pesticides.

Physical Demands

The physical demands described are representative of those that must be met by an employee to successfully perform the essential functions of this job. Reasonable accommodations may be made to enable individuals with disabilities to perform the essential functions.

While performing the duties of this job, the employee is regularly required to walk; use hands to finger, handle, or feel; and talk or hear. The employee frequently is required to stand, sit, and reach with hands and arms. The employee is occasionally required to climb or balance; stoop, kneel, crouch, crawl; and taste or smell. The employee must regularly lift and/move up to 25 pounds, frequently lift and/move up to 50 pounds, and occasionally lift/move more than 100 pounds. Specific vision abilities required by this job include close vision, depth perception, and ability to adjust focus.

Work Environment

The work environment characteristics described here are representative of those an employee encounters while performing the essential functions of this job. Reasonable accommodations may be made to enable individuals with disabilities to perform the essential functions.

While performing the duties of this job, the employee is regularly exposed to outside weather conditions. The employee is frequently exposed to moving mechanical parts. The employee is occasionally exposed to fumes or airborne particles, toxic or caustic chemicals, risk of electrical shock, and vibration. The noise level in the work environment is often loud.

Figure 8-2   (continued)

equipment and vehicles, lifting, and working outdoors would be listed under the physical requirements category; mental and emotional requirements would include working on multiple tasks, having good communication skills, and having the ability to cope with stressful situations. Nonessential functions are not listed to avoid being construed as discouraging disabled persons from qualifying for the position. For example, if a lawn mower operator is not required to lift heavy equipment, then lifting may be listed as a desirable, rather than as an essential, requirement.

Job titles are standardized within the company to ensure uniform job responsibilities and designations in the company structure.

> ■ Job titles are standardized to ensure uniform job responsibilities and designations. ■

As a company expands through diversification or acquisitions, the titles may be revised. Since job titles identify an individual's role, careful consideration is given to the title designation. In some organizations, salespeople are referred to as account executives, crew members as team members, operators as technicians, and foremen as supervisors. Human resource managers recognize this as something other than semantics since it enhances employees' self-image, which relates directly to their motivation and productivity.

Job descriptions have another essential function, which is to provide a profile of candidates for recruitment.

■ Recruitment

> ■ " 'People are your most important asset' turns out to be wrong. People are not the most important asset. The right people are." **Jim Collins,** *Good to Great* ■

Recruiting is a process by which companies attract the right persons for specific jobs. Recruitment emphasis in the landscape industry used to be primarily on management personnel until the advent of a labor shortage of field personnel. The industry projects, based on a conservative 3.5% industry growth rate over the next twenty years, that 600,000 new field employees will be needed by 2022. Newspapers no longer can be the primary resource for attracting them, and therefore a recruiting effort is necessary. Local employment agencies, religious institutions, high schools, and Hispanic media are contacted to recruit field labor. Financial incentives are often given to company field personnel to recruit employees. If the referral is hired and remains for a minimum period, the individual who recruited him or her is compensated.

The U.S. government's H2B program, until 9/11, had alleviated the shortage of field labor by providing a legal resource for migrant labor (see the section "Hiring"). However, immigration quota restrictions and demands by other service industries have made it difficult for many landscape companies to meet their field personnel requirements.

The recruiting process begins with management personnel who provide recruiters detailed descriptions of the positions they have available and the qualifications required. They also indicate traits and skills necessary to successfully fill entry-level positions and necessary to advance in the future. The recruiter then compiles the information into candidate profiles. A profile for a management position would include supervisory and organization skills, communication skills, self-confidence, people skills, and an extroverted personality. The jobs are posted on company Web sites and circulated among universities, community colleges, and technical schools that offer curricula in horticulture, landscape contracting/management, and landscape architecture. There are also several green industry search firms whose Web sites may list job postings. When interviewing candidates, the recruiter attempts to identify key characteristics that will enable individuals to attain success in their positions. Also, they will assess an individual's attitude to determine if he or she will fit in with the company culture.

Recruiters seeking entry-level management candidates are present at university and community college career days, industry trade shows, and the Professional Landcare Network Student Career Days, a national event attended by more than 800 college students from all regions of the country. The career day venue provides a medium for initial screening of candidates' qualifications and personality traits.

Selected individuals are subsequently invited to interview at the company headquarters. The recruiter uses the same management recruiting venues for hiring interns.

Additional recruiting efforts by TruGreen LandCare and other companies, vying for college graduates, include hosting recruiting weekends. Student prospects are invited to spend a weekend in the vicinity of regional or corporate offices. In this informal venue, the students have the opportunity to interface with management while becoming oriented to the company's culture and career opportunities.

■■ Internship Programs

internship programs
used as recruiting tools to find talented individuals who have the potential to become an integral part of management.

Internship programs are employed by the landscape industry to attract talented individuals who have the potential of becoming integral parts of the management infrastructure. The interns generally are employed for ten to twelve weeks during the summer. However, many companies offer internship programs year-round to provide interns with exposure to multiseasonal operations.

Internship programs require a major commitment by management at all levels to provide a learning experience for the interns. The company designates an internship coordinator who is responsible for the program structure and intern assignments. This person is critical to the success of the program as a monitor and developer of rotations or training modules to meet the needs of the interns and to develop potential employees. This is also the opportunity to develop mentoring skills in managers and supervisors.

The following guidelines provide direction for implementing a successful internship program:

- Provide academic institutions with detailed information regarding the program's orientation and expectations.
- Select a motivating coordinator.
- Provide flexibility to meet interns' specific interests, e.g., design/build, seasonal enhancements, irrigation, maintenance.
- Challenge the interns with projects that will enable them to apply, as well as develop, their skills.

The Brickman Group engages summer interns in enhancement projects. Under the direction of a project coordinator, the interns schedule client meetings, conduct a site analysis, develop an estimate, present a proposal to the client in a sales presentation format, and complete the installation of the project.

- Provide a venue for obtaining intern feedback.
- Select individuals as educational mentors.
- Incorporate field trips to nurseries, botanical gardens, and high-profile landscape sites.
- Expose the interns to local trade meetings.
- Include interns in division meetings.
- Provide competitive compensation.
- Arrange or subsidize housing for out-of-state students.
- Provide informal occasions for interns and employees to interact.

Interns are an excellent resource for new talent. Companies have the opportunity to evaluate their individual talents as well as their potential as supervisors and managers. If the program is well structured, interns often return for subsequent internships, enabling them to apply their previous experience to entry-level supervision in addition to broadening their experience through exposure to other divisions of the company.

An example of a landscape industry internship program is One-Source Landscape and Golf Services, which utilizes their client site at Busch Gardens in Tampa, Florida, to provide interns with a unique and horticulturally diverse learning experience. The interns are exposed to the latest developments in landscape management practices and have the opportunity to participate in numerous projects throughout the ten-week period. Areas in which the interns interface with staff include irrigation maintenance, seasonal color displays, turf management, pest management, sod installation, power equipment operation, and shrub maintenance, as well as general practices such as mulching, weeding, and fertilizing.

Chapel Valley Landscape Company in Woodbine, Maryland (Figure 8-3), determines the interests of first-year interns and provides them with a rotation through divisions that will enhance their skills. If students return for subsequent internships, they have the opportunity to fulfill their internship in a single division (for example, residential installation, maintenance, commercial installation, or irrigation).

Option I: Structured for the individual with limited hands-on experience.
- Two- to three-week rotation in commercial and residential installation and maintenance divisions.
- Emphasis on exposure to the industry through a variety of landscape projects.

Option II: Structured for the individual with at least six months landscape industry experience.
- Emphasis on knowledge and skill development.
- Individual selects one or two divisions for hands-on work experience.
- Additional experience is provided in business management through a one- to two-week rotation involving administrative projects. Individuals also have the opportunity to observe the role of management in daily decision making.

Figure 8-3   Chapel Valley Landscape Company Internship Program

Hiring

A primary concern in the hiring process, in addition to selecting the right person for the job, is to avoid legal problems. Employer guidelines include:

- State desired skills and experience in job descriptions.
- Word ads carefully.
- Require written applications.
- Be careful what you ask on applications to avoid discrimination, e.g. gender, age.
- Don't make casual promises.
- Get applicant's written consent to obtain information.
- Check references and previous employers.

Mistakes in hiring can result in costly legal issues. Companies can avoid stepping into legal traps by describing jobs in compliance with ADA regulations. As previously discussed, such compliance entails leaving out marginal or nonessential duties that may prevent a disabled person from applying for a position. Discrimination may become an issue if an ad is placed for a "salesman," which may be construed as excluding women. Reword the ad to ask for a "salesperson," or a "supervisor" rather than "foreman." Additional terminology that refers to age—"young" or even "energetic"—may be interpreted as discriminatory by the EEOC (Equal Employment Opportunity Commission).

Employment advertisements should not state preferred age to avoid charges of age discrimination by the EEOC.

Written applications are integral components of the hiring process. They provide a basis for documenting a candidate's qualifications. The applicant's signature on the application acknowledges that falsification of information will be grounds for dismissal. The signature also acknowledges, in an at-will employment state, a notification that employees can be dismissed without cause. References listed on the application should be authorized by the applicant, in writing, for permission to provide information. It is imperative that companies obtain additional information, such as credit checks, verification of academic credentials, driving records, police records, and previous job performance. Reference checks are important not only to verify performance but also from a safety standpoint. Drivers who are accident-prone will be a liability, and a person who has a violent background may injure someone who could sue the company for negligent hiring.

interview process
assesses an applicant's job qualifications through questions and tests.

The **interview process** can easily overstep legal boundaries, particularly since more than one interviewer is often involved. Interviewers should avoid sensitive areas such as marital status, children, health, age, race, or religion. Applicants may be questioned, however, about their ability to fulfill the job requirements and whether they would need special accommodations to accomplish it (for example, back support for clerical jobs). Medical exams for prospective employees are permitted by the ADA but only after a conditional offer of employment has been made. These exams must be required of all applicants, not just those who are disabled. Drug testing as a contingency for employment has become a common practice due to liability issues. This testing procedure must be enforced for all job applicants regardless of their position.

Another legal issue affecting the landscape industry pertains to the employment of immigrant labor. The landscape industry has been and will continue to be dependent upon immigrant labor. The federal government has initiated the H2B Program to assist companies. This program verifies immigrants' legal employment status before they enter the U.S. The H2B program classifies immigrants for temporary employment or training.

> ■ The H2B program classifies immigrants for temporary employment or training. ■

Immigrant labor in the H2B program are allowed to remain in the country for ten months. The temporary status specifies that the work is of a seasonal nature. A company acquires H2B employees after filing a petition with an INS (Immigration and Naturalization System) office. The petition is only granted if the company can validate that it is unable to fill its vacancies with U.S. citizens. Advertising the positions in the newspaper for three to four weeks fulfills this preapplication requirement.

Once the INS has approved the company's application for the work visas, either the company representative or a recruiting service (fee based) will bring employees into the country. The company is responsible for the employees' transportation costs and for locating a place of residence for them. Companies employing large numbers of H2B employees often acquire or build housing adjacent to their businesses, which they rent to the employees. Many companies have benefited from this source of labor, particularly those who have been fortunate to have 80% of the previous year's H2B employees return. The primary drawback to the H2B Program is the processing time. A 120-day period is required to file for employees. This requirement makes it difficult for landscape companies to anticipate their needs and to obtain employees when they are needed. Companies who apply for employees in November may not receive approval until March and then have to wait an additional thirty to sixty days for processing through the INS. However, this is the only program currently available, and in spite of the bureaucracy, it ensures that the employees are legally documented.

A company's hiring process is standardized with specific procedures to ensure avoidance of legal issues and to consistently hire the best qualified candidates. The pool of candidates generated through the recruitment process is subsequently interviewed by management personnel and a human resources manager/director (recommended for companies with more than 100 employees). A human resources manager is responsible for administering personnel matters such as hiring, processing seasonal/immigrant labor, disciplinary matters, termination, benefits, professional development, and providing company manuals.

The interview process (Figure 8-4) is focused on gaining an understanding of the candidate in regard to personal goals, strengths and weaknesses, and experience that would enhance job performance. Companies often have testing agencies conduct profile testing. This type of test is thought to reveal psychological traits, such as the ability to deal with stress and challenging situations as well as other behavioral patterns. Management candidates often are requested to take a more comprehensive test to evaluate leadership, management, and personality traits. These tests are analyzed by the testing agency and a performance rating is generated.

During the comprehensive interview, in which the candidate is asked specific questions pertaining to the position, a mutual decision may be reached regarding employment. The candidate is given a comprehensive understanding of the responsibilities associated with the position and his/her role as part of the company team.

Following an employment commitment, new employees are given an orientation by human resources personnel pertaining to company benefits and company policies, which are enumerated in the employee manual. The manual is a communication tool that enables employees to understand the company's philosophy and policies, the obligations and expectations of employment, company methods and procedures, and employee benefits. It also addresses essential legal items such as EEOC guidelines, affirmative action policies, COBRA (Consolidated Omnibus Budget Reconciliation Act) which provides individuals and their families the right to continue their group health plan for limited periods of time. Coverage is predicated on voluntary or involuntary job loss, reduced hours, job transitions, death, divorce, and sexual harassment complaint procedures.

I. Screening interview

II. Profile testing

III. Reference checks

IV. Comprehensive interview

Figure 8-4 Interview Process

■ Creating a Culture

The company that adopts the philosophy that employees don't work *for* their supervisors but rather *with* them has established the basis for a positive company culture. The manifestation of its effects will be readily evident in employees' attitude and productivity. At all levels, employees want to know that they are appreciated and are playing an integral role in the company's success. Respect, positive reinforcement, recognition, empowerment, professional development, compensation, and company events are the key building blocks for constructing a business culture that will attract and retain dedicated and productive employees.

How long employees remain with a company, as well as their productivity, is directly related to the relationship with their supervisor/manager. Employees don't leave a company, they leave managers. Employees who leave take their talents and training with them, often to a competitor. In order to attract and retain talented employees, company management needs to address the issues that are of primary concern to these individuals. These concerns, enumerated in "Measuring the Strength of the Workplace" (*First, Break All the Rules,* Marcus Buckingham and Curt Coffman), include:

1. Do I know what is expected of me?*
2. Do I have the materials and equipment I need?*
3. Do I have the opportunity to do what I do best?*
4. In the last seven days, have I received praise or recognition for doing good work?
5. Does my supervisor or someone at work care about me as a person?*
6. Is there someone at work who encourages my development?*
7. At work, do my opinions count?*
8. Does the mission/purpose of the company make me feel my job is important?
9. Are my co-workers committed to doing quality work?
10. Do I have a best friend at work?
11. In the last six months, has someone at work talked to me?
12. Have I had the opportunity at work to learn and grow?

*Most frequently cited among interviewed employees as links to retention.

> ■ "People don't change that much. Don't waste time trying to put in what was left out. Try to draw out what was left in; that is hard enough." ■

The manager's role is to motivate and develop each employee's talents, drawing out what is left in and thereby maximizing potential.

Successful managers have deviated from the norm regarding management style. A nonconventional or progressive manager approaches situations as follows, in contrast to a conventional style:

Conventional: Selects a person based on their experience, intelligence, and determination.

Progressive: Selects a person based on their talents and attitude.

Conventional: Sets expectations by defining the right steps.

Progressive: Sets expectations by defining outcomes.

Conventional: Motivates a person by helping him/her identify and overcome weaknesses.

Progressive: Motivates a person by focusing on his/her strengths.

Conventional: Develops the individual by helping him/her learn and be promoted.

Progressive: Develops the individual by finding the right fit, not necessarily the next rung on the ladder.

Talent is just potential; it takes managers to create an environment (culture) that allows talent to flourish. Progressive management defines the right outcome and lets each person find his or her own route to the outcome. An illustration of this concept would be a project manager who focuses on outcomes and avoids stopping and correcting each supervisor's management style. Defining outcomes encourages employees to take responsibility. This management approach places expectations on the employees while enhancing their self-awareness and self-reliance.

A basic human need is to feel appreciated. Recognizing this need and fulfilling it should be one of the primary objectives of a company culture. It can be easily achieved through positive reinforcement and recognition programs. Letters of commendation from the president of the company, employee-of-the-month recognition, and daily verbal recognition from supervisors instill a dedication and level of job performance that will exceed monetary compensation.

Recognition can take many forms, such as:

Tenure—years of service recognized with pins or certificates, monetary awards, gifts at a company event

Birthdays—cakes, personal greetings

Professional development training—leadership/technical training workshops

Division competition—recognition for attaining performance goals

Written recognition—notes or letters expressing appreciation

Safety awards—hours of service (crews) without accidents

Innovation awards—implementation of production efficiency ideas

Client satisfaction—acknowledgment from clients

Partners in excellence—annual selective criteria

Informal—daily acknowledgment

Formal—acknowledgment in front of peers and companywide

Awards—merchandise, gift certificates, dinners, trips, tickets to sports events

"By celebrating success we create a culture of success." **Disney Keys to Service Excellence**

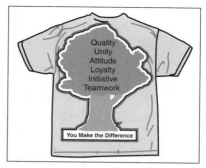

**Embossed on Company T-shirts,
Chapel Valley Landscape Company**

Recognition as listed above is often done at annual meetings, enabling all employees to recognize and honor their peers' accomplishments. This venue also serves as a motivating factor for individuals to strive to attain comparable recognition.

A fun environment also adds to a positive working environment. For example, one advertising agency would surprise its employees with a weekly mystery bus trip once a month. When the bus arrived, the office would be vacated and the employees whisked off to an amusement park, ball game, restaurant, and so on. The end product of a positive environment is a positive work force.

The Walt Disney Corporation has the following formula for business success:

Quality Cast Experience + Quality Guest Experience
+ Quality Business Practices = Success

The primary components that contribute to the success of this world icon are: selection (recruitment), training, communication, and care.

> The primary components of Disney management style that contribute to its success are selection, training, communication, and care of employees.

These components together comprise the Disney culture.

The Disney business culture is also comprised of standards in regard to job performance and client relations. Employees who feel part of a team and are motivated to perform their tasks will perpetuate these standards and the image that is created. The same principles hold true for a landscape company. The titles and job responsibilities differ, but the human elements are the same and so are the requirements: care, understanding, appreciation, and recognition as a team member. *Care* is a small word with a big meaning. All employees want to know that their employer cares about them as individuals and considers them an integral part of the company's success. The caring philosophy can be extended to the outdoor work environment: clean break rooms and restroom facilities, and a kitchenette for warming meals and storing food. Field personnel, who are often left out of the caring loop, will feel the positive impact of these efforts. Many landscape companies provide crew members with working attire for inclement weather and comfortable uniforms for warm weather, which is another significant caring attribute.

Jim Paluch, of JP Horizons, feels that development of a team-oriented culture starts with:

- Identifying what the employee enjoys doing within the company structure
- Determining the projects and tasks at which the employee excels
- Focusing on training employees in areas that they excel at and enjoy
- Enabling employees to serve as mentors as a means of attaining self-respect

This philosophy is manifested within many professions, including sports. Former coach John Wooden of UCLA basketball fame once said, "Do not let what you cannot do interfere with what you can do." The implication of this statement is that management should reinforce the positive attributes or strengths of employees rather than dwell on their weaknesses. An illustration of this point was expressed by football coach Lou Holz: "Put the right person in the right job now." He uses the example of a player who runs the 40-yard dash in 4.9 seconds, who is slow for the tight end position but fast for the tackle or guard positions.

Training and development is an important component of a company's culture, since it provides resources with which individuals can rise and succeed.

> ■ Training provides resources for individuals to rise and succeed in a company. ■

In every company, there are people with aspirations and talents that would enable them to be a greater asset, a faster player, if given the opportunity. In one landscape industry company, for example, a Hispanic employee was recognized by his supervisor for his perceptiveness and initiative. This individual was provided the opportunity to learn English and to be trained in his area of interest. Within a few short years, he became one of the company's top estimators and salespeople.

■■■ Employee Termination

Even in a tight labor market, employers terminate 15% of all new hires. The reasons are attributed to bad work ethics and attitudes and inadequate skills. The first approach to dealing with potential employee termination is to avoid it through counseling and monitoring.

> ■ Do not set termination as a goal. Strive for improvement in performance and behavior. ■

The goal is to improve the employee's performance or behavior. In these situations, the employer should:

1. Not set termination as the goal.

2. Achieve results by changing behavior or performance.

3. Find an alternative role that the employee can perform.

Federal and state governments now categorize more than 91% of workers into protected classes: minorities, women, people over 40, handicapped (inclusive of stress, obesity, high blood pressure, and perceived disabilities), pregnant, and adoptive parents. This broad protective umbrella provides a terminated employee with grounds for a lawsuit against the former employer.

If there is no alternative to termination, the manager should review the following guidelines:

Understand the situation—Analyze the basis for termination and check with human resources to verify justification. If downsizing, document the decision to do so and why a segment of personnel is slated for termination. Do not rehire an individual to fill a job category that will be abolished.

Employee manual—Does it have a policy procedure? Is there a warning process? In the event of an EEOC charge, the employee manual will be requested to verify if a policy has been violated. If an employee manual is not available, documentation will be accomplished through interviews and verification of past practices.

Examples of Employee Manual Policy Clauses

- **At-Will Employment**—States that the term of employment is not for a specific period of time and that it may be terminated at any time by the employee or company without reason, cause, or advance notice.
- **Equal Employment Opportunity**—Elucidates policy to provide equal employment opportunities regardless of race, gender, color, religion, national origin, age, physical or mental disability, medical status, marital status, veteran status, and sexual orientation.
- **Harassment**—States company's commitment to providing a work environment free of harassment associated with sexual orientation, gender, race, national origin, and age, physical or mental disabilities. Also includes a no tolerance harassment policy by non-employees with whom the company has a professional relationship. Defines what is encompassed by harassment and disciplinary actions that will be imposed upon those that violate the policy.
- **Complaints**—Procedures for filing and appeals.
- **Work Hours**—Daily work hours, breaks and lunch period.
- **Overtime Pay**—Compliance with state and federal regulations. Calculations on which weekly overtime will be based.
- **Resignation or Termination Payment**—When checks will be issued, predicated on the notice provided by the employee in the case of resignations. Termination payments are specified in terms of mail processing period.
- **Employee Benefits**—Who is eligible, when they are eligible for medical and life insurance in terms of period of employment, employee contribution and other benefits? Workmen's Compensation Insurance, Medical Insurance, Life Insurance, Retirement programs, tuition/course fee reimbursement.
- **Vacation, holiday, sick leave, maternity leave, family-care leave**—Lists the paid holidays that the company observes. Vacation and sick day accruals. Vacation scheduling and approval procedure. Stipulates eligibility and use of sick days and family-care leave.

- **Conflicts of Interest**—What constitutes a conflict of interest in regard to an employee's personal endeavors with those of the company?
- **Drug-free Workplace**—Defines substance abuse, disciplinary action, testing procedures, and effect of repeated offenses.
- **Employment Termination**—Stipulates violations and situations which may result in termination. Explains severance pay in terms of its applicability to involuntary termination.
- **Safety**—Company's commitment to maintaining a safe work environment. Provides safety guidelines and disciplinary action that applies to the infraction of them.

Union process—Were the contract provisions, grievance procedures, and appeals process followed?

EEOC considerations—Is there an existing affirmative action plan? How is the termination affected by the procedures associated with the plan? Is there documentation of all terminations over the last twelve to 12 to 24 months? Did the terminations include employees who were minorities, women, over 40, or disabled?

WARN (Worker Adjustment and Retraining Notification Act)—If there are 100 or more employees and 50 or one-third of the workforce was laid off, was a 60-day notice given and were local community officials notified?

Retaliation—Have any of the terminated employees filed lawsuits, EEOC charges, or grievances, which could be construed as retaliatory action?

Patterns—Are there intentional or unintentional patterns to the terminations, such as associated with health benefit coverage claims?

Consistency—Has the company been consistent in providing notices?

Severance pay—Is there a consistent pattern?

Documentation—Is a there chronological timetable of events leading up to the termination, such as noted on time sheets?

The termination process is done by the immediate superior, not by the human resources manager, who acts only if large numbers of employees are being terminated. The timing of the termination should be scheduled between Monday and Thursday before noon, never on Friday at 4:30, after a business trip, or before a holiday. The process should be direct, respectful, and considerate. The reason for termination should be expressed clearly and concisely, in a respectful and fair manner. The employee should be given an opportunity to respond, but this process should not offer a venue for disputing the termination decision. The employee may be offered the use of company resources, such as a fax machine and telephone, for a period of time for the new job search.

Following the termination process, the employee should be sent to the human resources department for an exit interview and further processing. The same applies for employees who have resigned. The exit interview enables companies to identify employment trends over a period of time and to establish a basis for management problems. The interviewer should be someone whom the employee views as impartial.

Examples of Exit Interview Questions
- How do you feel about the company?
- What was your working relationship with your supervisor?
- Was there sufficient training for your position?

TERMINATION FORM

Employee Information

Date of Termination _____   Social Security Number _____

Name   _____

Address   _____

City, State, Zip   _____

☐ I choose to voluntarily terminate my employment with (___Company Name___), effective _____

☐ Employee has been terminated due to lay-off, effective _____

☐ Employee has been fired, effective _____ for _____

_____

Employee statement   _____

_____

_____   _____

Employee signature   Date

Insurance Information

The law requires that under COBRA, (___Company Name___) offers employees continued health coverage under certain circumstances, including that the employee pay full monthly premiums in advance to (___Company Name___).

☐ I am not covered under the company's health plan.

☐ I am covered under the company's health plan, but do not wish to continue coverage.

☐ I am covered under the company's health plan, and would like COBRA coverage. (Additional form needed.)

Company Property Information

☐ Employee received no company property.

☐ The property detailed on the attached sheets has been returned in good condition to the company, and the employee has no responsibility.

Received by _____   Date _____

☐ The property listed below and detailed on the attached sheet HAS NOT BEEN RETURNED TO OUR COMPANY. Employee understands that payment for company property, as agreed, will be deducted from employee's final paycheck. In the event there are insufficient funds for full payment, employee agrees to pay the company in full for any balance due.

Property not returned _____

_____

Employee Signature _____   Date _____

Company Signature _____   Date _____

Figure 8-5   Termination Forms Record Pertinent Information Associated with the Termination Process

Source: Blueprint for Success, Professional Landcare Network, Herndon, VA.

- Was your job performance evaluation accurate?
- Did you feel that you were fairly compensated for your skills and responsibilities?
- Were you given opportunities for professional development?
- Did your supervisor provide positive reinforcement?
- Rate the following with excellent, good, fair, or poor: Company benefits, salaries, working conditions, management and supervision, advancement opportunities.
- What company changes would you recommend to improve employee retention?

EXIT INTERVIEW

Name _____ Date of hire _____

Social Security number _____ Last day of work _____

Position _____ Department _____

Reason for leaving _____

Ratings	Excellent	Good	Fair	Poor
Overall rating				
Company benefits				
Salary				
Working conditions				
Manager/Supervisor				
Advancement or training opportunities				
Other				

Additional comments on items above _____
_____

What specific circumstances led to this end of employment? _____
_____
_____

Would you consider, at some other time, working for our company again? Explain
_____
_____

Would you recommend our company to others for employment?
_____
_____

Describe your working relationship with your supervisor? _____
_____
_____

What advice would you give our company to prevent terminations in the future? _____
_____
_____

Figure 8-6 Exit Interviews Reflect the Working Environment from the Employee's Perspective

Source: Blueprint for Success, Professional Landcare Network, Herndon, VA.

The final step in the termination process is the issuance of a letter that states the date of termination without expressing reasons for the decision. Other employees who are directly affected by the termination should be notified, such as immediate supervisors. The employee's file should contain detailed records on the basis for the termination, a copy of the exit interview, and severance pay, if applicable. References may be given without legal concern if documentation can be provided for the respective statements.

Another legal concern with employee termination is a potential lawsuit that accuses the employer of preventing the individual from gaining future employment. A company can avoid this risk by the manner in which it disseminates information to reference inquiries. Information pertaining to confirmation of employment dates, title, salary, and whether the individual would be rehired, is safe ground from a legal standpoint. If the question is asked why the employee would not be rehired, a statement referring to company policy or job performance may be provided. If the future employer seeks more information, the company should request that the applicant sign a release authorizing further information to be given.

No law requires a company to employ someone who cannot do the job. Terminations are still a necessary part of doing business to ensure a company's future growth and development.

This chapter has covered a plethora of topics pertaining to acquisition and management of employees. The single most important concept that should be gleaned from the text is that employees are individuals who require cultivation, appreciation, and development, regardless of their position. The companies who cultivate their employees reap the harvest of growth and profitability.

 # Summary

How is employee identity established?

Teamwork among the employees at all levels, from field personnel to management, is essential to the growth and profitability of a company. The identity of team members is established with job descriptions. The job title and summation of responsibilities establishes the functional role of the individual in the company.

What are the components of job descriptions?

The job description enumerates qualifications, accountabilities, and tasks associated with the position. Management positions also have expectations stipulated in the position description.

The essential functions of the positions are presented in compliance with the Americans with Disabilities Act requirements pertaining to physical, mental, and emotional criteria.

What is the recruiting process?

The recruiting process focuses on attracting qualified individuals to a company. It entails using several resources ranging from the federal H2B immigration program to college career fairs, internship programs, and Web sites.

What legalities must be considered in the hiring process?

Hiring is a process that must avoid many legal pitfalls. The wording in job postings and ads must be in compliance with ADA regulations and abide by EEOC guidelines. The same legal concerns must be addressed during the interview process, such as avoiding issues of health, marital status, age, race, and religion. Newly hired employees must be provided with the company handbook and made aware of company policies such as grounds for dismissal.

What comprises a company culture?

The most important asset to the recruitment process is a positive company culture, one that maintains a caring environment for each employee and provides him or her the mentoring and opportunity to reach their maximum potential. Positive reinforcement from management involves accentuating the positive rather than the negative with the end result being increased productivity. Recognition programs that acknowledge achievement of personal goals through job performance and tenure are another manifestation of positive reinforcement in a company culture.

What is employee retention?

Employee retention refers to retaining employees for long-term employment. Companies that have been successful in retaining employees are those that have established a positive working environment. These companies regard their employees as assets and provide them the opportunity to attain their maximum potential.

What are the procedures for employment termination?

Employee termination is also a process that must proceed along legal guidelines. The first step in avoiding legal issues is not to set termination as a goal. Counseling and mentoring may be provided in an attempt to change an individual's behavior. It may also be possible to find an alternative position for the individual to better suit the person's talents and interests.

If termination is necessary, the following procedures should be followed:

- Chronological documentation pertaining to specific grounds for dismissal and counseling to allow for improvement
- Compliance with EEOC guidelines
- Reference to company manual grounds for dismissal
- Exit interview with the human resources department
- Termination letter

■ Knowledge Application

1. Write a job description, incorporating key components discussed in the chapter, for a position that you have held.
2. A potential applicant for a crew leader position enters your office with the assistance of crutches. What questions would you ask during the interview?
3. Describe a company culture that would influence your selection of an employer.
4. An employee was recently promoted to crew leader. Since his appointment, the efficiency of the crew has decreased, resulting in overruns on the budgeted time allocations. Would you terminate this individual? What factors would you take into consideration in reviewing this situation?

Productivity Basics

CHAPTER OBJECTIVES

To gain an understanding of:

1. Production factors

2. Production inefficiencies

3. Management's role in improving production efficiency

4. Employees' role in increasing production efficiency

5. Maximizing resources to increase productivity

6. Integrating technology into landscape production systems

KEY TERMS

communication

incentive programs

kaizen

PDCA cycle

process flowcharting

process management

productivity

quality standards

Productivity is a process that converts human and material resources into products or services. The efficiency with which this process is implemented determines a company's profitability. Payroll costs constitute the largest expense category on a landscape company's income statement. Attaining profitability, however, comes not from reducing the payroll expense but rather from increasing employee productivity.

productivity
a process that converts human and material resources into products or services.

"The key to productivity is not muscle power but brain power," said Frederick Taylor, an early twentieth-century businessman. Like the impact of robotics on mass production, the impact of mulch-blowing machines, leaf vacuums, and compact utility loaders have reduced muscle power and increased production efficiency in the landscape industry. The focus for achieving productivity efficiency is on working smarter rather than harder.

The landscape industry's emphasis on productivity is often directed toward field personnel, since they are performing the service that is sold to the client. In reality, productivity needs to be emphasized throughout the company since it affects every aspect of the company's operations. Management, administrative staff, sales, and estimating staff all have an impact on productivity. It is the brainpower throughout the company that enables the physical power to maximize production efficiency.

The Toro Dingo® Mechanizes Labor Tasks Thereby Reducing Costs and Increasing Productivity

Source: The Toro Company, Bloomington, MN.

■■■ Production Factors

In every job you have had, your performance has resulted in the production of a product or a service. Whether grilling hamburgers or mowing lawns, you knew what had to be done and what was required to get it done. You had a place to work and material resources to produce the end product or service—a cooked hamburger or a mowed lawn. In both job scenarios, a system existed with specific guidelines in place for you to complete the process.

The factors that contribute to a production process are illustrated in Figure 9-1. Production management provides the means for conversion of the input factors into a service. The efficiency of the entire process depends on what resources are available and how effectively they are managed to produce the service. The inputs are assets, which are the essential ingredients to implement the production process. Capital provides salaries and purchases the equipment and materials to provide the key components of the production process. These components are then incorporated into a production system that is structured to produce a service.

The competitive edge of a landscape company depends on the quality of its output and the amount of production hours required to produce it. The human element is the obvious key to achieving a company's production goal. Placing the right people in the right positions is critical to attaining production goals. Depending on the job position, companies may use tests to analyze an individual's traits and determine

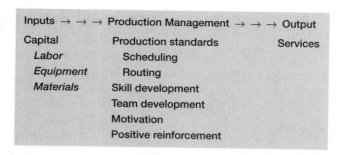

Figure 9-1 Production Process

strengths and weaknesses. There is a wide array of standardized tests that profile applicants and determine whether they would be a good fit for particular positions in management, sales, and so on. The tests match individual traits against profiles that are compiled after testing hundreds of people who are successful in their jobs. Some tests are also capable of determining an individual's energy level and compatibility. A sales profile would show a person who has a good self-image and an extroverted personality, is people oriented, and has strong communication skills. Management profiles consist of leadership traits, organization and communication skills, and most importantly, confidence in making decisions. What about field personnel? These individuals are placed according to specific company profiles that include a desire to work outdoors and the ability to tolerate adverse conditions, the physical ability to operate equipment and perform tasks, the willingness to be a team player, and the receptiveness to learn new skills.

Thorndale Landscape Company

Personality Test

	Agree				Disagree
1. When I enter a room I immediately engage in conversation.	5	4	3	2	1
2. I prefer to lead rather than follow.	5	4	3	2	1
3. I am team oriented.	5	4	3	2	1

A Useful Tool For Assessment of Leadership Potential and Compatibility in a Team-Oriented Environment

Management is responsible for the success of its production teams. It sets the parameters for the output and monitors the efficiency with which it is produced. Standards for company operations are communicated and emphasized in the training of production personnel. The managers and supervisors are the team leaders who create the production environment, provide the resources, and set the goals for the output.

■ Production Inefficiencies

Service businesses are time driven. The biggest challenge in providing those services is meeting the budgeted hours. Industry consultants have estimated that 35% of production time is wasted in landscape companies. Idle time or downtime (nonproductive time) can account for 15% of that time, most of which is wasted in the yard waiting for the crews to get their equipment and supplies for the day. Another example of time wasted is refueling vehicles, which idles an entire crew. Putting nonproductive time in perspective of lost revenue, a crew of three that is billed at a rate of $35.00 per hour and wastes 60 minutes per day will cost their company $21,000.00 annually in lost billable time (based on 40 weeks). Additional sources of lost production time occur with the following:

- Excessive travel time associated with poor routing
- Equipment breakdowns
- Return trips to the yard for materials, tools, and supplies
- Downtime while loading supplies
- Travel time to the job site
- Unskilled production personnel
- Lack of communication regarding budgeted hours
- Insufficient briefing on installation specifications

■ Production Management

A major portion of production management is associated with managing people. Managers need to be motivators and address the human factor rather than focus on the task-based factors. The fact that 19% of employees surveyed in a Gallup poll said that they felt disengaged at work reinforces this concept. These individuals work in a processing mode rather than focusing on results. The impact of disengagement on productivity is a loss of billions of dollars a year to employers. Motivating employees requires fulfilling their human needs and creating a working environment that will minimize their dissatisfaction.

> ■ Motivating employees requires fulfilling their human needs and creating a working environment that will minimize their dissatisfaction. ■

THEORIES OF MOTIVATION

Frederick Herzberg, in his research on employee motivation, developed a motivation theory that addressed minimizing employee dissatisfaction while simultaneously acknowledging employees and enabling them to advance within the work environment. The first part of his theory, called the hygiene theory, addresses factors that affect the work environment. All of the factors affect the satisfaction level of employees and their desire to achieve their maximum productivity potential. The extent to which management is cognizant of the employment impact of these factors determines whether a positive or negative work environment exists. These factors include:

Company Policies and Administration

- Policies communicated in a concise and comprehensible format
- Policies conveyed to employees with the goal of achieving understanding rather than intimidation

Supervision

- Emphasizing the positive rather than the negative, because positive thinking leads to positive results
- Providing opportunities for professional development; providing training to improve or acquire new skills; providing resources and training for certification exams, e.g., Professional Landcare Network Certified Landscape Technician, and Certified Landscape Professional, State pesticide applicator certification

Working Conditions and Interpersonal Relations

- Providing a clean and comfortable break room
- Providing the proper gear for adverse weather conditions
- Creating working relationships in which individuals feel that they are working with rather than for a supervisor
- Building a working team through trust and engagement in problem solving
- Instilling confidence and self-esteem by providing opportunities for self-accomplishment

Salary, Status, and Security

- Offering competitive salaries for comparable positions
- Offering compensation for advanced skills, experience, greater responsibility
- Offering reassurance that the company is financially sound and employees' jobs are secure
- Providing employees with a job identity and a sense of playing an integral part in the company's success

The second part of Herzberg's theory involves creating a work environment that will foster the following motivating factors:

- Achievement
- Recognition of achievement
- Interest in the task
- Responsibility for enlarged tasks and challenges
- Opportunity for growth and advancement to higher level tasks

Management style is critical to implementing the factors listed above. Employing a participative system is the most effective in fulfilling human needs. The entire team plays a role in decision making, which results in striving to attain goals and raise the productivity bar. When every individual feels he or she has made a contribution, all employees' levels of self-esteem and self-confidence are elevated.

A 2003 Dartmouth College medical study concluded that all humans are "hard-wired to connect." The study revealed that all of us have a need to communicate, to interact, to be motivated, and to motivate others. These results reemphasize the importance of addressing all employees' needs to motivate them toward a productivity goal.

Zig Ziglar, a motivational speaker, said, "People often say that motivation doesn't last. Well, neither does bathing, that's why we do it every day." This quote should be a screen saver on every manager's computer.

> "People often say that motivation doesn't last. Well, neither does bathing, that's why we do it every day." **Zig Ziglar**

Management Systems

Management systems are employed by companies to increase productivity, thereby improving profits and increasing customer satisfaction. Several articles and books have been written on the subject. Some are complex and require extensive training, others are more basic. The objective of any system, regardless of its complexity, is to get buy-in from all levels of personnel and to improve productivity efficiency. A brief synopsis of three systems follows.

TOTAL QUALITY MANAGEMENT

Total Quality Management (TQM) is an integrative system that is structured to provide improvement within the business environment in response to internal and external needs. The internal needs are in regard to improving company culture to meet the needs of employees and improve morale. TQM also addresses the human needs to attain job satisfaction, such as skill development and self-improvement. External needs refer to meeting customer needs such as quality and responsive service. The needs are identified through daily management and integrated into a system of improvement. Long-term goals are set in the business plan to:

- Improve employee morale, skills, and productivity
- Improve quality of services
- Increase customer satisfaction
- Improve customer retention
- Reduce production costs

SIX SIGMA

Six Sigma is a management system that requires extensive training and the assistance of business consultants. The name represents levels of improvement, with Six Sigma being the highest achievable. The system is based on a problem-solving method that focuses on increasing customer satisfaction and improving profits by increasing production efficiency and reducing production costs. The foundation of Six Sigma is measurable results based on statistical measurements.

Six Sigma teams, comprised primarily of senior middle management, are responsible for implementing process improvement. A process is defined as a sequence of steps associated with completing a task. The team members consist of the following:

Champion—a member of senior management whose responsibility lies with the logistical aspects and business principles of the process

Master Black Belt—who serves as a mentor to black belt team members, provides supports, reviews projects, and focuses on large projects

Black Belt—the team leader, who has the primary responsibility of implementing the Six Sigma process

Green Belt—an active participant in the project who engages in the implementation and application of the Six Sigma process

Process improvement refers to any business process, whether administration (e.g., invoicing) or field production (e.g., landscape installation). Every department is engaged in the improvement process. Priorities are given to those processes that have the greatest impact on customer satisfaction. Project criteria include:

- Clearly defined goals
- Project approved by management
- Manageable scope
- Project related to company mission

Team members pose the question, "How many mistakes do we make in the process?" After setting goals for the process—reducing downtime by 20%, for example—the team allocates resources to attain the desired goals. The team establishes the basis for the project by first justifying why it is a priority and deciding what its scope will be. It then proceeds to consider the following perspectives:

Financial—Which objectives will ensure the financial success of the project?

Customer—What impact will this project have on meeting customer objectives?

Internal—What process needs to be addressed to achieve the project's goals?

Educational—What do team members have to learn and implement in order to achieve the project's goals?

Results are measured to track the improvement of the variations implemented in the process. This measurement also reaffirms changes that have resulted in improvement and thereby ensures that the same results will be attained in the future. The number of mistakes that occur within a process gauges improvement. The level of improvement ranges from a low of One Sigma, which represents a 30% perfection level, to Six Sigma, which represents a 99.9% perfection level. The Three Sigma to

Four Sigma levels, which are within the 93% to 95% range, are where most companies generally plateau.

PDCA CYCLE

PDCA cycle
It is an easily implemented management system for addressing improvement in any aspect of a business operation through the application of planning, initiating, measuring, and implementing.

The **PDCA Cycle** (plan, do, check, act) is a pretty straightforward process that mimics the previous management systems in a more simplified fashion. The cycle employs the following sequence of steps:

Plan—Set a goal, e.g., reduce downtime by 20%.

Do—Initiate an action for improving a process, e.g., fuel and load trucks at the end of the day.

Check—Measure the results to assess the change in productivity efficiency, e.g., calculate the average crew downtime.

Act—Implement the new system through training and providing necessary resources. Determine whether additional action is required, e.g., designate individuals on a rotating basis to fuel and load trucks, or provide an additional pump on the premises to expedite the process.

As with all the management systems, the PDCA Cycle is an ongoing process, always setting new goals for improving the production processes.

Measurement indices serve as indicators of progress for everyone involved in the cycle.

> "People need to understand measurements in order to improve. You can't ask someone to lose weight without giving them a scale." **Professional Landcare Network Crystal Ball Report #23, 2002**.

Examples of indices are production hours for landscape operations compared to industry benchmarks, percentage of successful bids versus total submitted bids, percentage of contract sales versus sales calls, sales per full-time production employee compared to previous years, percentage of installation jobs completed on budget.

incentive programs
provide recognition and rewards for completing jobs efficiently.

Incentive programs, which are tied to measurable goals, are catalysts for increasing productivity and profitability. These programs provide recognition and rewards for completing jobs efficiently. The success of incentive programs is contingent upon selecting goals that are within employees' control. Examples of such goals are finishing a job in fewer than the budgeted labor hours, improving safety records, exceeding sales goals, reducing customer response time, reducing downtime, and exceeding budgeted financial goals. They will be effective in stimulating production efficiency if they are tied to team performance as well as to individuals. Peer pressure can be an effective means of getting buy-in from all individuals.

What types of incentives are effective catalysts? According to landscape professionals who gathered at a Professional Landcare Network Executive Forum, they are not necessarily tied to monetary awards. Individual or team recognition on a weekly or

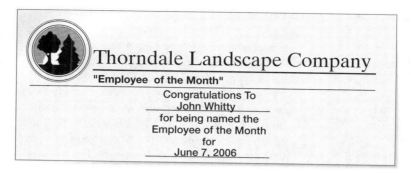

Thorndale Landscape Company

"Employee of the Month"

Congratulations To
John Whitty
for being named the
Employee of the Month
for
June 7, 2006

Recognition that Provides Positive Reinforcement

monthly basis, gift certificates, extra time off, or attendance at an industry conference may suffice as a reward for performance.

Improving Productivity

The best source for improving productivity is employees. They are engaged in their production roles on a daily basis, and therefore what better resource exists to determine how to improve a process? An individual (or a whole field crew) can be engaged in this exercise by outlining one of the processes and identifying the steps that could be improved to enhance production efficiency. This type of exercise is referred to as **process flowcharting.** The outcome of such an exercise is a detailed mapping of how the process is currently executed.

process flowcharting
outline a production process and identify the steps to improve it to enhance production efficiency.

Involving employees in the process lets them use their initiative to discover how the process may be done more efficiently. Their knowledge mostly likely comes from their experience but may also reflect knowledge of what is being done at another company. For example, an accounting employee told her company about a software program that her husband used to track equipment maintenance in relation to lifetime hours. This program determined the efficacy of repairing a piece of equipment based on its current hours of productive service. Implementation of the program saved the accountant's company repair costs on equipment that was at the end of its productive life cycle.

Productivity efficiency should extend beyond field production. Overhead costs can be significantly reduced through implementation of more efficient administrative processes. Such administrative processes may include:

- Contract processing time
- Invoicing time
- Expediency of posting payroll and invoices into the job costing system
- Processing time for accounts payable and receivable systems
- Customer inquiry or complaint response time

Regarding the above processes, human or technical resources may be limiting production efficiency. Informal surveys of the landscape contracting industry indicate that companies have one administrative employee for every million to million and a half dollars of revenue. This ratio is not a hard and fast rule, since the number of personnel is relative to their level of productivity. However, companies whose administrative personnel ratios deviate from those mentioned should quantify their productivity and determine whether they are over or understaffed. In this analysis, consideration should be also be given to the impact of technology, such as software programs on administrative production and to field technology, that would expedite data processing and thereby reduce the number of data entry personnel needed.

■ Process Management

process management
enables companies to compare the way a process was originally structured and how it is currently operating.

Process management enables companies to compare the way a process was originally structured and how it is currently operating. These processes are documented and discussions are directed toward identifying steps that can improve their efficiency.

Production teams may be asked to address how to reduce production hours for mulching, for example. Teams who have the lowest production hours for this operation can illustrate through their step-by-step outline how this is accomplished. In an open forum, production teams can benefit from seeing how other teams overcome roadblocks that lead to inefficiencies.

kaizen
a process that encompasses incremental improvement through the power and knowledge of those who are involved in the process on a regular basis.

This approach is similar to a process called *kaizen* used in Japanese industry. *Kaizen* encompasses incremental improvement through the power and knowledge of those who are involved in the process on a regular basis.

It relies on the knowledge and experience of these employees to identify where improvements are needed and to make recommendations for addressing them. Individuals on an installation crew may address crew size as an area in need of improvement. They might recommend that a crew size of three or four rather than six or eight would be more efficient, and further, that large jobs should have multiple crews, each with its own crew leader. In order for this process to succeed, each improvement needs to be:

Measured to assess time and quality factors

Monitored to assess efficiency and conformance to production standards

Improved wherever deemed necessary

quality standards
represent the parameters for a company's services.

Quality standards distinguish a company from its competition and are important in acquiring and retaining clients. Productivity improvement is, therefore, assessed on the basis of process efficiency within the respective quality standards. Jack Mattingly of Mattingly Consulting suggested developing a scorecard to periodically rate a production team. The scorecard breaks down the production process into its key components and rates each one on a point scale (Figure 9-2) The parameters for each component are predefined to remove subjectivity from the rating.

Landscape Installation

Site: _____   Supervisor: _____

Planting depth _____ (10)   Mulching _____ (10)
Rootball scoring _____ (10)   Watering _____ (10)
Bed edging _____ (10)   Pruning _____ (10)
Tree rings _____ (10)   Sodding _____ (10)
Staking _____ (10)   Cleanup _____ (10)

Deficiencies:

Scored by: _____   Date: _____

Landscape Maintenance

Site: _____   Supervisor: _____

Mowing _____ (10)   Weeding (beds) _____ (10)
Turf color _____ (10)   Weed control (turf) _____ (10)
Trimming _____ (10)   Deadheading _____ (10)
Edging _____ (10)   Cleanup _____ (10)

Deficiencies:

Scored by: _____   Date: _____

Figure 9-2 Productivity Standards Scorecard

Companies that have implemented process documentation have found that it is an effective means of identifying where roadblocks exist in a process and where breakdowns occur. When incorporated into the company culture, it serves as a reminder of what needs to be addressed to avoid inefficiencies that reduce productivity. All employees become proactive in seeking solutions for productivity improvement.

TRAINING PROGRAMS

Training programs are essential to productivity improvement. Employees who improve their skills or acquire new skills are capable of working more efficiently and productively. Their level of responsibility can be increased, and they become mentors for entry-level personnel. Training is also a motivator, since it advances the knowledge of employees and provides opportunities for their advancement.

Progressive companies are learning organizations. They are always seeking ways to become more efficient and productive. Some landscape companies require their employees to take a minimum number of education credits a year. The credits may be acquired through in-house training programs, community college courses, or workshops and seminars given by local or national trade associations, such as Professional Landcare Network, American Nursery and Landscape Association, International Society of Arborists, and the American Society of Landscape Architects.

Certification programs provide training seminars to prepare candidates for the certification exams. The Professional Landcare Network administers the Certified Landscape Technician and Certified Landscape Professional programs discussed in detail in Chapter 10. They require extensive preparation for application of skills and knowledge associated with interior and exterior landscape contracting. Some companies assign mentors to assist individuals in preparing for the exams. The end result of such programs is the elevation of professionalism in the field. These individuals become mentors for other production personnel and thereby establish an ongoing training program.

An effective mode of training is what is referred to as "just-in-time training." Information is presented to the employees just prior to when they can apply it. A pruning technique session on site prior to dormant pruning would be an example of "just-in-time training."

Safety and Operational Procedure Training Contributes to Production Efficiency

Source: The Brickman Group, Ltd.

Administrative costs account for a significant amount of a company's overhead and therefore warrant consideration as a training priority for enhancing production efficiency. Every administrative operation from payroll to contract processing can be addressed. An effective means of achieving administrative efficiency is through cross training. Cross training provides administrative personnel with new operational skills, enabling them to fulfill additional responsibilities. The benefits that will be derived include innovation by newly trained personnel who have an objective perspective of the new process and maintenance of productivity during the absence of key personnel due to illness, vacations, and attrition.

Cross training also has numerous applications to field production. Training installation and maintenance personnel in different production capacities enables them to work wherever they are needed for specific operations as well as being able to multitask on specific job sites. This additional skill training can serve as a motivator and a means of building self-esteem.

■■ Communication

communication

provides verbal clarification of production process.

Communication is also a vital entity to achieving production efficiency. Clear and concise communication between managers and supervisors ensures conveyance of expectations, current job status, and where improvements need to be implemented. Supervisors' communication with field personnel avoids misunderstandings and budget overruns from having to correct deficiencies in landscape operations. In addition, managers and supervisors affect productivity performance through daily positive reinforcement and recognition. The latter communication tools address the human factor, which relates to the need to be acknowledged and appreciated.

In today's landscape workforce, communication needs to be multilingual. Production processes must be instructed in the language of the crew members. Miscommunication often occurs when supervisors and managers are unable to convey instructions in the field. Productivity inefficiencies can be avoided through in-house training programs provided by college instructors or human resources personnel who are fluent

"Just-in-Time Training" Increases Productivity by Developing Multi-Task Crews
Source: The Brickman Group, Ltd.

in the languages spoken. The Professional Landcare Network and other trade associations have published books with Spanish phraseology pertinent to the Green Industry. Colleges offer Spanish immersion courses, which emphasize communication skills and comprehension of Hispanic culture. The latter engages the human factor: understanding a culture in order to address individuals' needs.

In addition, communication of skills and an understanding of the whys and the how tos will enhance productivity while elevating self-esteem. This pertains to conducting training sessions to convey the impact of maintenance and plant installation practices on the growth and development of plants, such as contrasting pruning with shearing and their effects on plant habits.

Productive communication is also achieved by maintaining a visual link with production schedules. These links are achieved by maintaining spreadsheets that reflect billable hours to actual hours, thereby revealing where inefficiencies occur and improvement is needed. Updating this data and providing copies to supervisors creates an awareness and impetus to improve productivity. Some companies post the information on job boards that reflect the budgeted hours to actual hours, such as mulching production hours listed by client with the actual hours expended. A combination of job boards and software spreadsheets will keep crews updated on their production status. Job boards are also used to post weekly and monthly job schedules. In the event of inclement weather, these postings enable adjustments to be made for labor and equipment allocations. The latter is particularly important for scheduling production sequences, such as fertilizing and mowing, grading and sodding, rototilling and seasonal color installation. Providing production crews with field job reports, budgeted hours, and materials and schedules provides communication links that will reduce downtime and improve production efficiency.

Communication is further enhanced with walkie-talkie systems and cell phones. A combined system, which is utilized by many companies, provides the benefit of convenient internal contact with management and other supervisory personnel. The latter contact is particularly important to reducing downtime associated with equipment breakdowns. The nearest crew can transfer equipment. If the company has a mobile repair van, it, too, can be contacted for on-site servicing. The combination of systems enables managers to be easily accessed by clients and vendors.

■ Equipment and Technology

Equipment in the landscape contracting industry is the most important mechanical entity for achieving production efficiency. Breakdowns are the nemesis of production hours. Stringent maintenance programs and backup inventory reduce the downtime associated with breakdowns. If a company doesn't have in-house maintenance, then backup inventory is critical to avoid job delays due to slow turnaround from repair shops. Replacing heavily used equipment every three to four years affects production by providing the latest developments that will make job processes more efficient and thereby reduce labor hours.

The advent of zero turn radius mowers adds versatility to the mowing operation and reduces the number of hours associated with trimming. Mowers with chain rather than belt drives have substantially reduced required maintenance. Compact utility loaders like the Toro Dingo® provide versatility in landscape construction. One machine that has the capability of digging ponds, lifting trees, transporting sod, and digging or auguring holes for planting trees eliminates a substantial number of work hours as well as workers' compensation claims for strained backs. Power bed edgers enable crisp edges to be achieved without the need for shovel edging. They are also versatile enough to cut in tree rings. Contracting or purchasing mulch blowers greatly enhances productivity in large areas where wheelbarrows would normally be used to transport mulch to beds and tree rings. Leaf vacuums not only increase productive efficiency over raking and bagging, but they also reduce the leaf debris to approximately one-tenth of its volume. The finely ground leaves can either be directly applied to beds or placed in compost piles to increase the nutrient value of the final decomposed product.

Technology is being employed by the landscape industry to improve the production efficiency of operations in administration and field production. It has proven to be an asset for increasing accuracy and facilitating estimating, measuring, and accounting. Various design software programs have proven to be visual sales tools. Examples of specific applications are discussed here.

CLIENT PRESENTATIONS

Digital imaging and 3-D design programs provide tools that enable clients to visualize landscape designs in perspective and on their residential or commercial footprint. User-friendly programs provide a database of plant materials and hardscape materials which can be utilized to generate a conceptual landscape design with an actual digitized image of the client's house or commercial complex. More sophisticated programs interface digital imaging with AutoCAD, providing a more realistic perspective of a landscape and in a multidimensional format.

FUEL CONSUMPTION

Computerized fuel pumps provide accurate records of fuel costs for production vehicles and equipment. Coded cards are required to activate the system, which provides a database of the date and amount of fuel consumed. This information can be downloaded to the server to be incorporated into job costs for specific client accounts. In addition, this technology reduces downtime, since crews are not standing idle and spending nonproductive time in a gas station convenience store.

SOFTWARE SYSTEMS

Laser fiche programs permit scanning of business documents, such as client files, estimates, or contracts, and storing them in a computer file in a PDF format. Doctors' offices utilize this system to scan thousands of patient files, reducing the space required for file storage and increasing the efficiency of retrieving the information. The same application is pertinent to the landscape industry. Contracts, estimates, and other documents can be retrieved from the files at the touch of a keyboard.

Personal digital assistants (PDAs) have multiple applications in the field. They can be used to record labor hours for each job site. Crews are signed on and off as they arrive and depart from job sites. Estimators can generate estimates using estimating programs. Supervisors can access job schedules and daily or weekly field reports specifying job details and budgeted labor hours. Invoices can be generated and printed on a portable printer. All of this information can be accessed and downloaded from a home computer.

Rainbird® markets a PDA program called Rainbird Pro® that uses Hindsight® software. The software is compatible only with Palm Pilots® that have at least 8 MB of memory and PCs with Windows® 98, 2000, or XP. This system can schedule irrigation installation or maintenance jobs, control inventory, control, and update work orders. Irrigation crews that have utilized this system have eliminated at least four hours a day associated with filling out time cards with imprecise data, updating work orders, and checking inventory in their trucks. The latter is accounted for in the program for each part used, thereby providing a current inventory of irrigation parts on the vehicle.

When a client calls the office, a work order is generated, which is then downloaded to the PDA by service personnel from their home computer via a modem. The service crew always has updated work order information and security codes to access and service the property. Invoices can be produced on site, printed on a portable printer, and then left with the client for immediate payment. At the end of the day when the service crew signs off, the PDA clocks them out and automatically bills the client. Service personnel then download all work order information from their home computer to the company server. This process keeps the accounting department current with all completed jobs, which expedites client billing.

Another feature of the software is routing crews based on zip codes. This increases efficiency in terms of reducing travel time and customer response time. Emergency calls also can be updated into the PDAs. GB Sprinklers of Des Plaines, Illinois, has experienced increased productivity of office personnel since using Rainbird Pro®. The company found that the invoicing that used to take eight hours to process could be accomplished in one hour.

Gravely®, a manufacturer of lawn mowers, developed the Eye-Q® productivity system for the lawn care industry. The electronic data system assists landscape management companies to increase productivity efficiency through analysis of operators' productivity, monitoring equipment maintenance and analyzing the mower's performance. The system is comprised of an electronic component that interfaces with an electronic data system. This component assists in reducing downtime by communicating the current operating status of the mower and the maintenance schedule to ensure its efficient operation (Figure 9-3).

The Eye-Q® system accomplishes operating efficiency by:

   Tracking the equipment maintenance needs

   Providing access to maintenance logs and parts required for servicing

   Detecting component failures and warning of dangerous operating temperatures

   Providing real-time troubleshooting of the electrical system

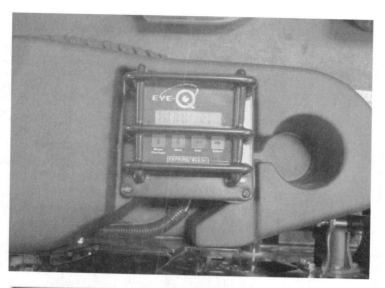

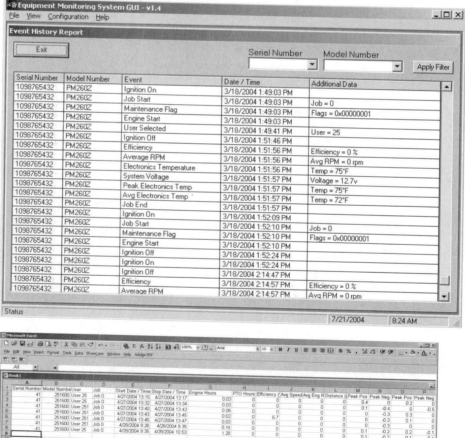

Figure 9-3 Eye-Q® Monitoring System

Source: Ariens Company, Brillion, WI.

Customizing a maintenance schedule based on the specific landscape and environmental needs

Using sensors to detect trends in decreased performance, e.g., dull blades or the need for engine service

Maintaining a log of all the maintenance performed for the mower

Alerting mechanics to servicing needs, e.g., tire pressure, lube, belts, deck leveling, oil

The Eye-Q® system also provides features that enable monitoring of the operator's productivity:

Records time and site location during equipment operation

Relays budgeted time to actual time used

GPS records location automatically, and monitors cutting speed and distance traveled for each job and operator

Displays individual hours for ignition time and engine time

Shock sensor detects if equipment is being used efficiently

Displays time functions continuously

An option of the system enables downloading data via a wireless remote module. This module, named Scanmate®, allows the data to be uploaded into a PC. Managers and mechanics can readily access the information to monitor current job productivity and mower maintenance.

The development of this technology will undoubtedly lead to similar components being incorporated into other equipment such as skid steers, front end loaders, trenchers, and so forth. The data obtained will provide landscape contractors with pertinent information for refining their production processes and increasing their profitability.

Adding sophisticated technology to landscape equipment also will serve as a motivating factor for equipment operators. The operator's job will acquire an elevated status with the added responsibility of data management. Training programs will provide the operators with the knowledge to assess the equipment and their respective productivity while monitoring the equipment maintenance for peak performance. These individuals can then function as individual production efficiency managers for their equipment. Having immediate access to current productivity levels also will assist in setting goals. Recognition of goal achievement is possible from daily downloading of the data.

The Global Positioning System (GPS), which was developed for the U.S. military, utilizes satellite signals to establish latitude and longitude. This system can detect ground locations within 300 feet. Since its deregulation in the 80s, this location system has been adapted to a multitude of businesses. The landscape industry is one of the latest business sectors to implement this technology into production systems. Landscape companies equip their trucks with GPS units to add another efficiency quotient to their productivity formula. The system provides information on:

Arrival and departure time from job sites—providing accurate information on time spent on the job and between jobs. It provides verification records to validate invoices and thus reduces the downtime associated with unscheduled stops.

Location of vehicles—facilitating transferring equipment to other crews and directing mechanics needed to make on-site repairs.

Travel speed—reducing safety risk, particularly with trailers.

Routing—providing updated directional information to reduce travel time and avoid downtime due to construction sites and direction errors. The system can reroute crews in the event of emergencies, client requests, or cancellations. Interfacing with a routing software program enables maximizing route densities and determining where deviations occur from the scheduled route. Routing efficiency reduces travel time and thereby increases productive time.

Linking the GPS unit with a networking feature called MRM (Mobile Resource Management®) expands the system to become a communication link with field personnel.

There are two types of GPS MRM systems, passive and active. The passive system collects the data and downloads the information at the end of the day. The unit can be removed for this process, or the data can be transmitted via an antenna mounted outside an office building. The active system provides constant communication links and transfer of information. This system enables wireless communication via e-mail between managers and crews, thereby providing personnel management. Last-minute client requests can be transmitted as well as any problems that are occurring onsite. Since the GPS is web based, managers can track the progress of their crews while remaining at their desk computer. If the crew is exceeding allocated time, the manager can determine what the problem is and convey a solution to the field supervisor. If it is a case of needing equipment or materials, the manager can arrange for securing whatever is necessary without involving downtime by having personnel leave the job site.

The productivity benefits of the GPS systems are:

 Accurate accounting of production labor hours

 Time management, since crews are cognizant of their production time

 Efficient means for managers to monitor productivity

 Reduced fuel costs due to routing efficiency

All of this technology requires a significant capital investment for the hardware, software, and monthly service charges (for active systems). However, based on productivity improvements and fuel savings, GPS system suppliers claim an ROI (return on investment) of over 300%.

CHEMICAL SYSTEMS

Plant growth regulators (PGRs) are chemical tools that are utilized by the landscape contracting industry to increase production efficiency. Their primary function is to reduce growth of turf, shrubs, and trees. Secondary functions include eliminating turf

Class	Growth Response	Landscape Application
Gibberellic acid inhibitors	Reduces stem elongation	Turf, shrubs, trees
Cell division inhibitors	Reduces plant growth	Turf, shrubs, trees
Ethylene enhancers	Prevents fruit formation	Shrubs, trees

Figure 9-4 Classifications of Plant Growth Regulators

seed heads and undesirable fruit set on ornamental trees. When incorporated into landscape management programs, PGRs have a significant impact on the reduction of labor hours associated with mowing and pruning. The classes of plant growth regulators that have application in the landscape industry are listed in Figure 9-4. Figure 9-5 lists the effects of using PGRs.

The plant growth regulators alter plant growth through their effect on the plant's biochemistry. The classes of PGRs listed have three distinct modes of action, restricting the synthesis of plant hormones such as gibberellins and cell division compounds, and enhancing the production of ethylene. Ethylene is often referred to as a ripening agent or maturation compound.

PGRs are most frequently used to manage turf on golf courses and large commercial sites. Lawnscapes of Ontario, California, evaluated the management impact of a growth regulator on a 165-acre site. After one year's application, the growth rate of the turf was reduced by 50%, resulting in a 26-week reduction in the mowing schedule, a 60% reduction in clippings and dump fees, reduced wear and tear on equipment, decreased fuel and equipment maintenance by approximately 50%, and a 20% reduction in water consumption. This company's use of a PGR enabled it to utilize its crews from 26 weeks of mowing to enhancing the appearance of other landscape entities.

Lawnscapes' net gain from PGR use:

Client satisfaction and retention—Reallocation of mowing time to landscape detailing, reduced water bills

Reduction of overhead—Lower equipment maintenance and fuel costs, fewer dump fees, and less downtime

Reduction of job costs—Fewer labor hours for clipping removal

Plant growth regulators are a production management tool. It is not a tool that will necessarily have application to every job, and where it is applicable, the justification should be based on an economic assessment. Management needs to determine whether the material and application costs provide sufficient savings in labor and equipment costs to incorporate PGRs into a client's contract. One of the key cost determining factors is the length of the growth control period and the company savings during this period.

The basics of productivity are people related. How people are managed, trained, and motivated determines the amount and quality of their production. Providing employ-

Turf	Reduced cutting cycles, trimming, and edging
	Reduced thatch buildup
	Reduced water consumption
	Increased stress tolerance
	Restricted broadleaved weed growth (e.g., spurge, henbit, oxalis, clover)
	Transitions turf from annual rye to warm season grasses
	Suppresses *Poa annua* growth
	Restricts seed head formation
	Enhances turf seedling establishment through suppression of established turf
	Increases turf density among stolon and tiller turf types
	Improves color and appearance
Shrubs	Restricts shoots and terminal growth surges
	Enhances branching and shrub density
	Reduces or eliminates flowering and fruit formation (e.g., privet, multiflora rose)
Trees	Restricts terminal growth
	Reduces or eliminates undesirable fruiting (e.g., olive, crabapple, sweet gum)
	Removes mistletoe shoots
	Prevents seeding of mistletoe

Figure 9-5   Growth Management from Plant Growth Regulators

ees with the latest developments in equipment and technology elevates the level of production that can be achieved. The key to productivity is management of a company's human assets.

◼ Summary

What are production factors?

The production process consists of three primary factors: input, production management, and outputs. The most important input component is labor, based on the impact on the quantity and quality of output. Production management is the manner in which the labor component is managed and provided with production resources. Production management is the catalyst for production efficiency.

What are some of the primary production inefficiencies?

The most consistent production inefficiency associated with the landscape industry is downtime or nonproductive time. This inefficiency is associated with delays in crews leaving the company yard, fueling, and routing. Additional inefficiencies are associated with equipment breakdowns and inadequate training of field personnel.

What is management's role in improving production efficiency?

Management is directly responsible for identifying areas of production inefficiency and determining what is necessary to correct the situation. Rerouting or reassigning job sites could reduce travel time; reassignment of mower sizes used on job sites may increase efficiency; mechanizing tasks, e.g., with utility loaders, also may increase efficiency. Most importantly, management is responsible for motivating production personnel through positive reinforcement, recognition, and professional development.

What is the employee's role in increasing production efficiency?

Employees are the gears that turn the production wheels. Their role is to perform their tasks in the most expedient manner while maintaining company standards. Each of them has the responsibility of identifying inefficiencies and becoming a part of the solution. The solution may require training and development and/or additional resources, such as new equipment.

How can resources be maximized to increase productivity?

By management's analysis of the inefficiencies and identification of the resources required to correct the inefficiencies. Engaging personnel in analyzing landscape operations through a system such as the PDCA Cycle will aid in the identification of inefficiencies and the implementation of corrective measures to increase productivity. Corrective measures that address time management, development, motivation of human resources, and provision of required material resources will produce the output desired: increased productivity.

How has technology been integrated into landscape production systems?

Computer technology has had the most significant impact on the landscape industry. Real-time job cost reporting, estimating systems, and software for PDAs have increased efficiency and productivity. Additional applications include production of landscape designs and presentations, automated time-card entry, and equipment maintenance monitoring. The use of GPS units has further enhanced productivity through tracking, routing, and job cost management. Plant growth regulators are chemical tools that facilitate landscape management. This class of chemicals includes growth retardants, pruning agents, and flower and fruit inhibitors.

■ Knowledge Application

1. List four distinct production-related deficiencies that you have observed, e.g., service related such as city or county public works, restaurants, landscape maintenance companies, or college dining services.

2. Apply the PDCA Cycle to a landscape maintenance or installation operation.

3. Describe a company culture that would motivate you to maximize your productivity potential.

4. Outline an incentive program for increasing production efficiency within a landscape maintenance company.

Professional Development

CHAPTER OBJECTIVES

To gain an understanding of:

1. Professional development goals

2. Professional development resources

3. Multilevel development training programs

4. Integrating professional development into the company culture

Whether it is referred to as training or skill development, the goal is the same: to provide employees with professional development. Professional development is applicable to all positions within a company. The landscape industry could not have evolved to its status today without educational training acquired through seminars and workshops and from consultants. As companies evolved from pickup truck operations to multimillion-dollar corporations, owners recognized the necessity of instituting internal and external training programs. The impetus for expanding these programs is driven by a competitive market that necessitates maximizing the potential of human assets.

Companies that succeed develop their human assets. These employees perform at high levels of competency and are proactive in improving the productivity and efficiency of their team. Professional development is an ongoing process that perpetuates a company's growth and profitability.

No one will dispute the fact that there is a direct correlation between training and productivity. Regardless of the level of one's education or professional experience, there are daily reminders that "you don't know what you don't know" (Landon Reeve, Chapel Valley Landscape Company). It is therefore imperative that companies continually take the opportunity to offer their employees learning venues that will benefit their

HGIC's Plant Diagnostic Web Site

Welcome! The University of Maryland, Home and Garden Information Center's Plant Diagnostic Web Site offers photographic keys to help diagnose and solve plant problems, using Integrated Pest Management principles.

Development of this site is made possible by grants from the Chesapeake Bay Program and the Northeast Regional IPM Grants Program, which is funded primarily by the U.S. Department of Agriculture (USDA) with additional support from the Environmental Protection Agency (EPA).

Please give us feedback through the online Survey. We will continue to expand the site, so visit again soon!

For site directions and basic IPM information please choose from the list below:
Site Directions
Instructions for Submitting Plant or Insect Samples
Developing Diagnostic and Decision Making Skills.
Non-Chemical control Strategies for Pests and Diseases.
How to Decide When to Take Action Against a Pest, Disease, or Environmental Problem.

MARYLAND Integrated Pest Management

Web Site Credits   Last Update 12/03/04   Web Master

Note: This site is best viewed at a resolution of 800x600 with 256 colors or better using Netscape 7.0 or higher. Apple users will have best success viewing this site with Internet Explorer 5.0 or Netscape 7.0.

Web Access to University Agriculture Extension Sites Provides Resources for Plant Diagnostic Training

Source: University of Maryland Cooperative Extension.

professional development. Within the landscape industry, there are several venues that provide opportunities for acquiring skills and knowledge:

- Trade associations that conduct conferences and workshops:
    Professional Landcare Network
    Professional Grounds Management Society
    American Nursery and Landscape Association
    International Arborist Association
    American Society of Landscape Architects
    Regional landscape contractor associations

- Manufacturers' technical representatives that offer training:

    On site

    Local seminars/workshops

- Consulting firms

    On site

    Regional seminars/workshops

- Publications

    Periodicals

    Trade association journals

    State Agricultural Extension bulletins

    Horticulture Research

- Web sites

    Trade associations

    University Agricultural Extension

    University/college long-distance learning

    Internet search engines

- Courses

    University Agricultural Extension

    Universities and community colleges

■ Trade Associations

trade associations

are comprised of member businesses in the same industry.

Trade association conferences are one of the best resources for professional development. They provide an opportunity to learn from industry leaders and consultants on subjects ranging from financial management to water management. One of the largest conferences, attended by thousands of landscape contractors, is the Green Industry Conference (GIC). Trade associations coordinate the conference: Professional Landcare Network, and the Professional Grounds Management Society (PGMS). This learning venue also provides an opportunity to network with industry peers for an exchange of ideas and mentoring. Informal breakfast and lunch meetings, as well as receptions, provide an informal format for exchanging information. An example of such a format is "Breakfast of Champions" at the GIC. The champions are industry leaders who address specific topics in round-table discussion groups. Topics cover human resources, financial management, sales and marketing, leadership, design/build installation, maintenance, irrigation, and arboriculture (see Figure 10-1).

The external professional development resources do not replace in-house training programs, but they are an important adjunct to the whole development process. Individuals attending conferences and workshops come back inspired with new ideas and are enthusiastic to see the results of implementing these ideas. The return on investment

Executive Management	Middle Management	Field Supervisors
Defining leadership	Managing a multicultural labor force	Water conservation principles
Hiring, inspiring, retaining a labor force	Profitability through productivity	Lawn pesticides
Risk management strategies	Cutting-edge sales techniques	Perennials, ornamental grasses
Communicating a business vision	GIS/GPS mapping systems	Landscape diagnostics
Open book management	Client management	Color in the landscape
Smart growth marketing		Training the trainer

Figure 10-1 Examples of Conference Topics

The National Green Industry Conference Provides Many Opportunities to Network and Access Information About the Landscape Industry
Permission granted by the Professional Landcare Network, Herndon, VA.

Trade Shows are an Excellent Venue for Networking and Acquiring Equipment and Supply Vendors
Permission granted by the Professional Landcare Network, Herndon, VA.

from those attending far exceeds the investment associated with travel and conference fees. Motivation, improved job performance, and employee retention are some of the dividends derived from this form of human asset development.

■ Seminars and Workshops

Seminars and workshops conducted by business consultants address an array of subjects to provide personal and professional development. The workshops are structured to engage registrants in interactive exercises so they can apply their newly acquired knowledge and skills. Examples of these workshops are:

The Training Advantage conducted by JP Horizons:
- Human resource skill building: recruiting, hiring, coaching
- Just-in-time training program development
- Time management skill building

Leadership Jam by JP Horizons:
- Leadership development:
    Goal setting

    Team building

    Communication

    Planning

    Delegating

    Thrival Campaign

Programs such as Thrival Campaign train workshop participants to utilize a structured approach to attain results. The workshop provides a template or guide that employees can utilize to achieve specific goals. An example of an application of Thrival Campaign is illustrated in Figure 10-2. The campaign's goal is to develop 100 viable leads for expanding sales. A sales manager would engage the sales team in the action steps that would lead to the campaign's defined goal. Time lines and team member responsibilities would be established for each step of the campaign.

■ Training Programs

training programs

provide a venue for improving employee skills.

Training programs are an integral part of a company's culture because they are directly responsible for increasing productivity and efficiency. Just as important as the end result of these programs is that they represent a company's commitment to its employees. A comprehensive series of training programs for all levels of employees provides them with the knowledge and skills required for advancement. The benefits to

training investment

returns dividends in employee productivity and retention.

the company from its **training investment** are manifested in the employees' productivity, morale, empowerment, ability to make decisions, and retention. Retention of trained employees provides the company with a competitive edge, since their work

Campaign: 100 Viable Leads

Specific result: Develop a team-oriented program to find viable leads to pursue.

Dynamic Action 5: Establish 100 leads and track the business they generate. Celebrate team's achievement.

Dynamic Action 4: Assign team members to lead focus areas: former clients, drive-bys, networking, e.g., apartment associations, property management companies, homeowner associations, existing clients.

Dynamic Action 3: Select a leader to direct the campaign. Develop a lead sheet.

Dynamic Action 2: Conduct a campaign orientation, discussing the format, process, and how to generate leads.

Dynamic Action 1: Develop an action plan that includes a lead sheet, a tracking database, and a posted campaign progress chart.

Figure 10-2 Thrival Campaign

Source: "Leadership Insights," JP Horizons, Inc., *Landscape Management,* August 2003.

manifests quality, consistency, and efficiency. A company's financial success hinges on its team of quality employees. Landscape companies generally target a 75% retention rate of field personnel, 85% of field supervisors, and 95% of managers.

Successful training programs are contingent upon the program structure and the ability and knowledge of the trainer. Trade associations and consultants offer seminars and workshops to develop trainers' skills. Kraft Associates/ODA Inc. conducts training seminars based on the K.A.S.H.© system: training programs that develop employees' knowledge, attitude, skills, and habits. The titles of these seminars, "Training the Trainer," have become a cliché in the industry. The common objective of these seminars is to provide participants with the skills necessary to conduct an effective training program. The skill topics encompass:

- Communication
- Organization
- Instructional materials
- Role playing
- Program evaluation
- Reinforcement

Retention of information conveyed in a training program depends on the delivery format. This point is evident by results of comprehension studies that have been done on the amount of retention from reading, hearing, seeing, speaking, and doing:

Retention Rates—

10% reading

20% hearing

30% seeing

50% seeing and hearing

70% speaking

90% doing

If plant identification was the training topic, a CD or Web format would need to be supplemented with plant samples. That would fulfill the "doing" aspect of learning, handling and examining live plant samples. Engaging trainees in learning plant identification techniques at a job site, nursery, or arboretum would certainly reinforce the training objective.

In addition to knowledge retention, other important factors that contribute to effective training programs are:

Scheduling—convenient for the audience

Duration—the average attention span is twelve minutes, so three topics can be covered in a half-hour session

Consistency—weekly, monthly, seasonal

Content—emphasis on application versus theory

Bilingual—all verbal instruction and instructional materials need to address the multicultural labor force

"Just-in-time" training—information presented on site for immediate application

Manuals—to illustrate and emphasize the topic

The infrastructure of a training program for field personnel consists of a series of customized subject modules that address topics which have a direct impact on production efficiency. Examples of training modules for landscape maintenance and installation divisions are presented in Figure 10-3.

Many topics can be introduced into a company's training program, some of which can be delivered in daily "just-in time" situations and others over longer periods of time. Incorporated throughout the training programs are the company's standards and its commitment to constantly improve its services through the professional development of its employees.

Regardless of the level of training, the trainer's mode of information dissemination is directly related to the comprehension and retention of the trainees:

"Tell me—I'll forget."

"Show me—I'll remember."

"Involve me—I'll understand."

These statements reiterate the previously mentioned retention rates, showing that an individual's act of doing reinforces the learning process. They also add another dimension to the act of doing: comprehension. California Polytechnic State University is an icon for the learning engagement process. Cal Poly's academic environment combines theory with practice. The institution clearly articulates its philosophy in its motto, "Learn by Doing." Regardless of the teaching venue, classroom or job site, trainee interaction is imperative.

Maintenance Division

I. Equipment Operation
   a. Operation procedures
   b. Safety
   c. OSHA requirements
   d. State Department of Transportation regulations
   e. Maintenance
   f. Troubleshooting

II. Turf Management
   a. Mowing height
   b. Edging and trimming
   c. Aerating
   d. Fertilizing
   e. Weed identification and control
   f. Pest and disease control
   g. Diagnostic skills
   h. Irrigation system maintenance

III. Shrub Management
   a. Pruning techniques
   b. Plant identification
   c. Pest and disease control
   d. Bed edging
   e. Weed control

IV. Pesticide Application
   a. Material safety data sheet
   b. Environmental Protection Agency requirements
   c. State agricultural agency regulations
   d. Equipment calibration
   e. Pesticide mixing procedures
   f. Application techniques
   g. Sprayer cleaning procedures
   h. Chemical spectrum of activity
   i. Phytotoxicity symptoms
   j. Diagnostic skills

Installation Division

V. Plant Installation
   a. Plan/blueprint interpretation
   b. Plan take-offs
   c. Specifications
   d. Site analysis
   e. Equipment operation
   f. Safety
   g. Site preparation
   h. Planting procedures
   i. Change orders
   j. Plant establishment procedures

VI. Irrigation System Installation
   a. Design interpretation
   b. Site analysis
   c. Equipment operation
   d. Safety
   e. Manifold installation
   f. Pipe and sprinkler installation
   g. Controller installation
   h. Controller programming
   i. System troubleshooting and maintenance
   j. Winterizing system
   k. Spring startup procedures

Figure 10-3   Training Modules for Landscape Maintenance and Installation Divisions

Input	Action	Output
Training plan	Training program	Production
Scheduling		

Reinforce/Modify	Evaluate	Feedback
Review training	Results: expected versus actual	Measure productivity
Modify training	Impact	Quantitative
	Clients	Qualitative
	Employees	
	Company	

Figure 10-4   The Training Loop

Source: K.A.S.H.© A System of Training, Kraft Associates/ODA, Inc.

The training process doesn't stop at the end of the session. Monitoring, evaluation, and reinforcement are also part of the process. These phases of the process assess the impact of the program and determine whether supplemental training is necessary. The "training loop" in Figure 10-4 represents the phases associated with the training program cycle.

■ Certification Programs

certification programs

qualify individuals for a professional status based on their application of knowledge and skills.

Certification programs have been developed by national and state trade associations to elevate the professional standards in their fields. Training materials are available through these associations, and they offer regional seminars and testing sites. Landscape companies use these programs to advance the knowledge and skills of their employees. Attaining certification is regarded as a significant step in an employee's professional development and most often is tied to financial incentives.

The Professional Landcare Network administers two certification programs: the Certified Landscape Technician (CLT-Interior/Exterior) and the Certified Landscape Professional (CLP-Interior/Exterior).

CERTIFIED LANDSCAPE TECHNICIAN (CLT-EXTERIOR)

This certification test consists of two sections, a written problem-solving section that addresses installation and maintenance situations and a hands-on section that tests skills within specific modules (candidates select one module).

PROBLEM SOLVING

First aid and safety	Irrigation controller programming
Reading landscape plans	Plant identification
Sod installation	Work orders and reports
Irrigation component identification	Truck and trailer operation
Tree planting, staking, guying	Chainsaw operation

Hands-On Modules*

Installation	Maintenance	Irrigation
Plant layout	Pruning	Reading plans
Grading and drainage	21" mower operation	Lateral installation
Survey instrument	Walk-behind mower operation	Main line installation
Paver installation	Riding mower operation	Valve repair
Rototiller operation	Pesticides	Valve wiring
Tractor/skid steer operation	Fertilizers	Pipe installation—trencher
	Aerator operation	Pipe installation—puller
	Blower operation	

*Each module also has a written comprehension component.

CERTIFIED LANDSCAPE PROFESSIONAL (CLP-EXTERIOR)

The CLP test is restricted to candidates who are business owners or managers. Its development resulted from a collaborative effort between the Professional Landcare Network and the Professional Development Institute. Certification candidates are tested on subjects associated with business management.

Business planning	Sales
Accounting	Marketing
Management	Communications
Liability risk	Public relations
Contract law	Human resources
Safety	Production operations

Training is an ongoing process at all levels of employment. The success of training programs is contingent upon the commitment of owners and managers. This commitment should be based on the assumption that people want to excel at what they do. Developing employees through such programs improves production quality and efficiency and provides individuals with job satisfaction.

■ Summary

Training adds value to a company's human assets. Providing structured programs develops employees' skills and provides them with challenges and increased self-esteem. Production efficiency and quality is enhanced and perpetuated at all levels.

What are professional development goals?

Professional development goals are those that are directed toward maximizing the achievement potential of a company's human assets. These goals should be inclusive of all employees from upper management to field personnel.

What are some professional development resources?

Sources for external training venues include:

Trade association workshops and seminars

Certification programs

University extension workshops and courses

Trade conferences

In-house training programs incorporate "just-in-time" training for on-site instruction and implementation of production practices. The key to the success of these programs is structure, consistency, and duration. The infrastructure of these programs consists of training modules, e.g., on equipment safety, turf management, pruning, and so on. In-house training resources can be supplemented by outside technical representatives.

What are multilevel development training programs?

Multilevel training programs address the skill levels required for advancement to higher level positions. These programs may require outside resources, e.g., leadership workshops, financial management seminars, and possibly courses at community colleges or universities.

How can professional development be integrated into a company's culture?

Professional development should be a component of every company's culture, since it is one of the primary factors associated with employee retention and productivity. Management can establish mentors for "just-in-time" training and provide opportunities for individuals to participate in external training and certification programs. On-site training sessions can be conducted with instructors from local colleges or the community. Business consultants also are a resource for on-site training.

A company's investment in training programs provides dividends in the form of employee empowerment, job satisfaction, retention, and production efficiency.

■■■ Knowledge Application

1. As an entry-level landscape manager, what type of training would you expect to receive?

2. Structure a "just-in-time" landscape training module for an installation or maintenance operation.

3. List six professional development resources offered by one or more of the following trade associations:

   Professional Landcare Network, www.planet.org

   American Nursery and Landscape Association, www.anla.org

   International Society of Arborists, www.isa-arbor.com

4. Review the following Web site for horticultural information that has application to "just-in-time" training of landscape field personnel: www.agnr.umd.edu. Click on "producers." List training topics that could be developed from this information.

Bottom Line Leadership

CHAPTER OBJECTIVES

To gain an understanding of:

1. Positive leadership traits

2. The effect of leadership on employee motivation

3. Leadership's role in employee development

4. Leadership values

When all is said and done, leadership stands out as being the one determining factor in a company's financial success. It all begins at the top with executive management's vision and structuring of the company. Once the company's infrastructure is defined, it will only move forward in a competitive market with strong leadership. There are examples in the landscape industry of those who have led and those who haven't. Companies that personify strong leadership have grown from a small cadre of employees to hundreds and from revenue of thousands to millions of dollars. Chapel Valley Landscape Company, whose founder and former president, Landon Reeve, started out in the 70s with 50 employees, today has over 350 and is still growing. The Brickman Group, Ltd., started out in the Chicago area and today is a national corporation with over $400 million in sales. This type of growth is not related to an infusion of capital; it is directly related to leadership.

Throughout this book, the human factor has been defined as the key to success in the landscape industry. Equipment doesn't get the job done, people do.

Equipment doesn't get the job done, people do.

Equipment doesn't produce a profit, people do. The motivating factor that is the catalyst for production and profit is leadership—leadership that permeates the entire company.

Leadership is the catalyst for production and profit.

A company's culture evolves from the president of the company. Positive company cultures create a work environment of motivated and productive employees. These are employees who wake up in the morning and look forward to going to work. Companies with this type of culture thrive because of their level of productivity and efficiency. Their success comes from retaining employees whose experience and leadership are constantly improving the company's bottom line.

Financial management builds and maintains the framework for the company's production. It tracks production history and establishes parameters to ensure that current and future production achieves profit goals. This aspect of management is critical to the survival and future growth of all companies. However, regardless of the degree of financial management sophistication, it's production efficiency and production volume that generate black ink on the bottom line. These two production factors are prevalent in companies with "contented cows."

■ Results-Oriented Leadership

Two books that are must reads on the subject of leadership are *Contented Cows Give Better Milk,* by Bill Catlette and Richard Hadden, and *Fail-Safe Leadership,* by Linda Martin and Dr. David G. Mutchler. They both clearly define leadership and relate its impact on the business world. Both books address the need to create a working environment that motivates and meets the needs of employees.

For ten years, profitability and revenue comparisons were made with "contented cow companies" and their industry peers. In all instances, the "contented" companies were consistent in profitability and exceeded the revenue of their industry rivals. Among the top 50 landscape companies that appear annually in *Landscape Management,* a trade journal, how many hold their ranking from year to year? The answer: All of them. Does this mean that they are "contented cow" companies? There certainly must be some level of contentment in these organizations that enables them to attain their level of sales revenue. The best way to retain a loyal customer base is through establishment of a fully engaged workforce.

> The best way to retain a loyal customer base is with a fully engaged workforce.

The results that every company is seeking are increased sales, productivity efficiency, and profitability. All of these results are people driven and strongly dependent on leadership. This requires leadership that:

- Motivates employees to work faster and more efficiently
- Sets high expectations
- Empowers employees by providing information resources
- Listens to its people

- Cares about its people—"If you care you're there"
- Develops people

■ "Contented people give better performance." **Tommy Lasorda** ■

■■ Company Vision and Mission

"Contented companies" not only meet the leadership criteria previously stated, but most importantly, they engage every employee in fulfilling the company's vision. This vision is expressed in a vision statement that describes the future, where the company is going, or where it wants to go.

An example of such a statement is manifested by the Birmingham chapter of the Red Cross: "To be recognized as a compassionate organization setting the standard for alleviating human suffering." The Brickman Group Ltd. expresses its vision through the following statement: "To provide the highest level of service and quality to our customers while striving to be a learning organization that works constantly to improve." Vision statements provide a foundation for employee commitment and understanding of management's perspective of the future.

Mission statements focus attention on essentials and summarize the core competencies and capabilities of the business. Together, mission and vision statements provide direction for a business by focusing attention on doing things day-to-day to accomplish the mission while taking steps to pursue the vision.

A mission statement complements the vision statement by expressing the basis for the company's existence and how it will pursue its vision. An excellent example of such a statement is that of the American Red Cross: "The American Red Cross is a humanitarian organization, led by volunteers, that provides relief to victims of disasters and helps people prevent, prepare for, and respond to emergencies. It does this through services that are consistent with its Congressional Charter and the principles of the International Red Cross Movement."

■ Vision statements describe a company's future direction. Mission statements summarize a company's core competencies and capabilities. ■

Everyone is on the same page and knows where the company is going. Once everyone knows the path the company is traveling, they can determine what they can do to help it reach its destination. Mission statements foster a team-oriented environment, enhance employee morale, and provide everyone with a clear company image.

A company's leadership is a sustaining competitive advantage—leadership that knows how to set goals and achieve desired results. Leaders are guides showing the way while simultaneously directing employee performance that is necessary to reach the company's destination. These leaders set high expectations that result in high performance. They make people feel powerful rather than making them feel powerless.

This goes along with having high expectations and assigning people responsibilities that instill confidence in them. Individuals on the receiving end will have the desire to prove that having faith in them is well founded.

■ Multilevel Leadership

One primary characteristic of effective leadership is knowing when to lead and when to follow. Once the direction is established, effective leaders develop their people, empower them with the necessary resources, and motivate them to achieve to their highest level. The direction is defined in terms of the desired results; for example, sod installation within a specified number of hours and to installation specifications. In addition, effective leaders develop the processes that are necessary to ensure the desired results. In the landscape industry, this would apply to operating procedures and standards, such as for tree installation and staking. Effective leaders do not micromanage, nor do they suppress innovation and problem solving at any level.

■ Effective leaders know when to lead and when to follow.

Leadership is all about results, and development is about creating a working environment in which all individuals recognize their role and responsibility in achieving the goals to which they commit. People must be empowered with processes that allow them to lead. When this is accomplished, everyone in the organization becomes a leader. Multilevel leadership results from empowerment, providing a company with decision-making depth. Just like a basketball team with a strong bench, each player knows what it takes to win the game. This team of leaders will be motivated to set positive examples, serve as mentors, and perpetuate a team culture.

Two great leaders expressed their perspective of leadership in a very similar vein:

■ "Don't tell people how to do things, tell them what to do and let them surprise you with their results."   **George S. Patton**

■ "The best executive is the one who has sense enough to pick good men* to do what he wants done, and self-restraint to keep from meddling with them while they do it."   **Theodore Roosevelt**

*Today Teddy would have referred to people.

■ Summary

Leaders have the responsibility of developing and motivating individuals to perform to the best of their ability. Leaders influence the working environment and are responsible for motivating individuals to accomplish their goal in the most efficient manner. When this is achieved, a company has a competitive advantage, because "contented cows give better milk."

Production quality and quantity are increased by leadership that:

- Motivates individuals to become more efficient in their jobs
- Sets high expectations
- Supports rather than impedes
- Listens
- Empowers individuals by providing training and information resources
- Cares about its people: "Lead by your heart"
- Develops leaders

Positive results come from positive leadership.

■ Knowledge Application

1. Select a landscape operation and define how multilevel leadership can enhance attainment of the desired results.
2. What skill development would strengthen your leadership qualities?
3. What impact does leadership have on the work environment and the end results?
4. Describe an existing company that personifies innovative leadership.

Business Principles of Landscape Contracting

Landscape-Related Trade Associations

Educational and Training Resources

References
  Business Management
  Leadership

Landscape Trade Journals

Templates
  Operations-Scheduling Installation
  Installation Project Planning Checklist
  Production Sheet
  Job Cost Sheet

Pricing Examples
  Maintenance Services
  Mowing Prices
  Topsoil
  Mulch

Financial Statements
  Installation Balance Sheet
  Maintenance Balance Sheet
  Installation Income Statement
  Maintenance Income Statement

■ Landscape-Related Trade Associations

American Nursery & Landscape Association
1000 Vermont Avenue, N.W., Suite 300
Washington, D.C. 20005-4914
(202) 789-2900
www.anla.org

International Society of Arboriculture

www.isa-arbor.com

The Irrigation Association
8260 Willow Oaks Corporate Drive, Suite 120
Fairfax, VA 22031-4513
(703) 573-3551
www.irrigation.org

Professional Grounds Management Society
720 Light Street
Baltimore, MD 21230
(410) 752-3318
www.pgms.org

Professional Landcare Network
950 Herndon Parkway, Suite 450
Herndon, VA 20170
(800) 395-2522
www.landcarenetwork.org

Sports Turf Managers Association
1027 S. 3rd Street
Council Bluff, IA 51503
(712) 322-7862
www.sportsturfmanager.com

Tree Care Industry Association
3 Perimeter Road, Unit 1
Manchester, NH 03103
(603) 314-5380
www.treecareindustry.org

■ Educational and Training Resources

American Nurseryman Publishing Company
223 W. Jackson Blvd., Suite 500
Chicago, IL 60606-6904
(800) 621-5727
www.amerinursery.com

Professional Landcare Network
950 Herndon Parkway, Suite 450
Herndon, VA 20170
(800) 395-2522
www.landcarenetwork.org

Multimedia Educational & Training Resources
San Luis Video Publishing
P.O. Box 6715
Los Osos, CA 93412-6715
(805) 528-8322
www.horticulturevideos.com

Horticulture Education
P.O. Box 9
102 Hwy. 81 North
Calhoun, KY 42327-0009
(800) 962-6662
www.nimcoinc.com

American Nursery & Landscape Association
1000 Vermont Avenue NW, Suite 300
Washington, D.C. 20005-4914
(202) 789-2908
www.anla.org

■ References

BUSINESS MANAGEMENT

Blueprint for Success
Professional Landcare Network
950 Herndon Parkway, Suite 450
Herndon, VA 20170
www.landcarenetwork.org

Guide to Growing a Successful Maintenance Business
Guide to Growing a Successful Installation Business
Professional Landcare Network
950 Herndon Parkway, Suite 450
Herndon, VA 20170
www.landcarenetwork.org

Pricing for the Green Industry, 2nd ed.
Frank Ross, Ross/Payne & Associates, Inc.
Professional Landcare Network
950 Herndon Parkway, Suite 450
Herndon, VA 20170
www.landcarenetwork.org

How to Price Landscape and Irrigation Projects
James Huston
J. R. Huston Enterprises, Inc.
P.O. Box 1244
Englewood, CO 80150-1244
www.jrhuston.biz

Landscape Estimating and Contract Administration
Steven Angley, Edward Horsey, and David Roberts
Delmar Thomson Learning
3 Columbia Circle
P.O. Box 15015
Albany, NY 12212-5015
www.delmar.com

Operating Cost Study
Professional Landcare Network
950 Herndon Parkway, Suite 450
Herndon, VA 20170
www.landcarenetwork.org

LEADERSHIP

Contented Cows
Bill Catlette and Richard Hadden
Satillo Press, TN

Fail Safe Leadership
Linda L. Martin and Dr. David G. Mutchler
Delta Books, FL

First, Break All the Rules
Marcus Buckingham and Curt Coffman
Simon & Schuster, NY

Leadership and the One-Minute Manager
Ken Blanchard
William Morrow and Co., NY

Who Moved My Cheese?
Spencer Johnson, MD
G. P. Putnam's Sons, NY
www.whomovedmycheese.com

■■ Landscape Trade Journals

American Nurseryman

www.amerinurseryman.com

Landscape Management

www.landscapemanagement.net

Lawn & Landscape

www.lawnandlandscape.com

Landscape Construction

www.lcmmagazine.com

Landcare News

www.landcarenetwork.org

Landscape & Irrigation

www.abm.net/post/

Tree Care Industry

www.treecareindustry.org

Turf

www.turfmagazine.com

Templates

Operations—Scheduling Installation

Job Name

Job Number

Supervisor

Estimated hours to date

Actual hours to date

Revised date

Description	Site Preparation		Irrigation Installation	Tree Installation	Sod Installation
Est Qty					
Est Hrs					
Hrs/Unit					
Unit Price					
Total Job to Be Billed					
Est Hrs Date					
Mat Used Date					
M					
T					
W					
Th					
F					
Sat					
Week Total					
Weekly Billing	$	$	$	$	$

An Operations-Scheduling Report Provides Supervisors with Real-Time Job Status

Source: Blueprint for Success, Professional Landcare Network, Herndon, VA.

INSTALLATION PROJECT PLANNING CHECKLIST

Date _____ Contract # _____

Client Name _____ Contract # _____

Address _____ Salesperson _____

City, State, Zip _____

Contract Amt: _____ JMA Amt. _____ Subcontract Amt. _____
(amount sub charges)

Sub-Sold Amt. _____
(amount JMA charges)

Total Hours _____ # of Days _____ Amount $/Day _____

Date	Initials	
		Receive accepted proposal
		Make up schedule board tags (1 per day)
		Set up contract in accounting system
		Create project hours estimate by operation
		Print the following job reports:
		A. Production Sheet—2 copies
		B. Shipping Ticket—1 for each day
		C. Plant Only List
		Log information on contract spreadsheet
		Log information on production report spreadsheet
		Log information on subcontractor spreadsheet
		File original proposal and estimate in client file
		Assemble production packages as follows

PRODUCTION PACKAGES ASSEMBLY

Office Copy	Superintendent	Foreman	Plant Tagger
This Cover Sheet	Cover Sheet	Cover Sheet	Plant Only List
Bid	Production Sheet	Production Sheet	Perennial Order Form
Proposal	Proposal	Proposal	Lighting Request Form
Plan	Plan	Plan	
Map	Map	Map	
Any Special Forms	Any Special Forms	Any Special Forms	
Processing Form	Processing Form	Processing Form	
	Shipping Ticket	Time Sheets—1 per day	
	Project Info Sheet	Extra Sheets	

A Project Manager's Planning Punch List that Sequences To-Dos

Source: Blueprint for Success, Professional Landcare Network, Herndon, VA.

PRODUCTION SHEET

Customer # _____   Bid Date _____

Name _____   Site _____

Address _____   Address _____

City, State, Zip _____   City, State, Zip _____

Description of Operation	Unit of Measure	Qty.	Equip. Hours	Labor Hours	Supervisor Hours	Total Hours

A General Production Sheet that is Applicable for Summarizing Maintenance or Installation Operations Associated with Specific Jobs

Source: Blueprint for Success, Professional Landcare Network, Herndon, VA.

JOB COST SHEET

Customer _____   Site _____

Address _____   Address _____

City, State, Zip _____   City, State, Zip _____

Bid Date _____

Labor Rate _____   Super Rate _____   Sub Margin _____   Labor Ovhd _____

Super Ratio _____   Degree of Diff. _____   Mat'l Ovhd _____   Profit Margin _____

Item/Description	Unit	Qty.	Cost	Extended

SubTotal

Net Profit

Total Estimate Price

An Estimating Form for Pricing Job Operations

■ Pricing Examples

MAINTENANCE SERVICES

Misc. Landscape Price List

Minimum Price for Team to Visit Customer's Property	$89

Lawn Mowing — See mowing price list on reverse

Weed Beds by Hand — $65 per man hr. for one-time weeding. For regular weeding of mulch customers, use 35% of mulch price (pre-emergent weed control and mulching are prerequisites) If mowing customer, we weed every visit If non-mowing customer, we weed every third round

Rototilling SF	Lawn area (To make a bed or garden)	Garden area (To cultivate existing garden)
0–549	$89	$89
550–699	16¢ SF	$89
700–899	15¢	$89
900–1,149	14¢	10.0¢ SF
1,150–1,449	13¢	9.0¢
1,450–1,799	12¢	8.5¢
1,800–2,199	11¢	8.0¢
2,200–2,649	10¢	7.5¢
2,650 + up	9¢	7.0¢

Weed & Feed
- **(under 1/2 acre)** — 1.75 x mow price (per application)
- **(1/2–1 acre)** — 2.00 x mow price (per application)
- **(1–2 acres)** — 3.00 x mow price (per application)
- **(2-1/4+ acres)** — 4.50 x mow price (per application)

Shrub Trimming — $65 per man hour for trimming, cleanup & bagging debris $75 per man hour for renovation pruning, which requires cutting back 50% or more of the shrub, often requiring use of a chain saw
Flowering = May (best); Non-Flowering = Sept. (best)

Tree Pruning — $75 per man hour for pruning, cleanup and either dumping debris in woods or loading on trailer

Hauling Tree Debris (and Any Large Quantity of Yard Waste) to Landfill — if debris cannot be dumped in woods
- $135 for up to 1/3 trailer load
- $195 for up to 1/2 trailer load
- $269 for full-to-overflowing trailer load

Clean Beds — $65 per man hour (incl. bagging or dumping in adjacent woods) for removing leaves, weeds and grass

Edge Beds — price per linear foot

	If debris can be dumped in woods	If debris must be hauled away	
Beds currently have a decent edge - any LF	.80 LF	.80 LF	Circle box titled "Haul All
Little or no edge present - 500+ LF	.90 LF	.90 LF	Brush to Landfill" and
Little or no edge present - 1–499 LF	1.00 LF	1.00 LF	enter price of $77
Tree rings with decent edge present	$25/ring		
Tree rings with no edge present	$30/ring		

Stripping Sod (& leaving debris on site in adjacent woods)
| 1–299 SF | $1.00 SF |
| 300 + up SF | $ .90 SF |
If debris must be hauled away, circle box titled "Haul All Brush to Landfill" and enter price of $83

Fertilize Shrubs & Trees — 25% of mulch price

Pre-emergent Weed Control — 30% of mulch price

Mulch Beds — See mulch price list. (Determine # of bags needed & divide by 9 to get # of cu. yds. needed)

Spring Yard Cleanup — $50 per man hour for cleanup & bagging debris or dumping in woods If debris must be hauled away, circle box titled "Haul All Brush To Landfill" and enter price of $98.

Edge Concrete Walks, Curbs & Driveway — $.30 per LF (if turf has grown well over concrete) $.04 per LF (if edging has been done fairly recently) } "One-time-only" pricing
See bottom of Mowing Price list for edging with mowing.

Gutter & Downspout Cleaning — See gutter cleaning price list

Grind Tree Stumps — See stump grinding price list

Install (bury 6" deep) — 10' sections of black plastic perforated drainpipe at base of downspouts $98 per section ($9.80/LF for longer lengths)

Fall Leaf Removal — $50 per man hour for cleanup and A) Bagging debris if under 12 bags leaves or B) Dumping leaves in adjacent wooded area $89 for truck vac (if over 12 bags of leaves, and removal from site is required)

Annual Colorscaping
- For Summer – Install flats of annuals during 1st wk. of May (15 4-1/2" pots per flat) — $54 per flat (most annuals)
- For Summer – Install flats of annuals during 1st wk. of May (15 4-1/2" pots per flat) — $69 per flat (specialty annuals*)
- For Fall – Install 8" pots of mums during 3rd wk. of Sept. — $9 per pot
- For Winter – Install 8" pots of cabbage or kale during 1st wk. of Nov. — $9 per pot
- For Winter – Install flats of pansies (15 4-1/2" pots per flat) during 1st wk. of Nov. — $54 per flat
- For Spring – Install tulip bulbs – $1.25 each or install daffodil or hyacinth bulbs – $1.50 each during 1st wk. of Nov.
- * Non-stop Begonias, Caladium, Double Impatiens, Wave Petunias, Zonal Geraniums, Gerbena Daisy, New Guinea Impatiens

Lawn Seeding Options

	Under 1/2 Acre	1/2–1 Acre	1–2 Acres	2-1/4+ Acres
Good	5 x one cut	6 x one cut	8 x one cut	10 x one cut
V. Good	10 x one cut	12 x one cut	16 x one cut	20 x one cut
Excellent	15 x one cut	18 x one cut	24 x one cut	30 x one cut
Premium	20 x one cut	24 x one cut	32 x one cut	40 x one cut

Late March Thru Early April = great time; September = best time

Cutting Back Perennials — Usually Oct./Nov. or Feb./March — $65 per man hr. using string trimmer and leaf rake

Cutting Back Ornamental Grass — Usually Feb./March — $65 per man hr. using shrub trimmer and leaf rake

Install Landscape Timbers — (not more than 3 tiers high) using 1/2" rebar to secure timbers (Always add $60 to price determined using calculations below. Price incl. removing and replacing existing soil.)

1st Tier	4 x 4 = $9 LF 6 x 6 = $11.50 LF	**2nd Tier**	4 x 4 = $9 LF 6 x 6 = $11.50 LF	**3rd Tier**	4 x 4 = $9 LF 6 x 6 = $11.50 LF

An Example of a Company's Pricing for Maintenance Services

Mowing Prices — Year 2004

Size property incl. house, driveway, pool, etc. (excluding woods)			Price to MOW, TRIM, EDGE & BLOW a NORMAL LOT (For lots requiring extra time, see footnotes)				Price Per Man Hr. is based on the average cut taking	
			Can cut at least 92%+ with a	Price	Equivalent to Charging			
					Per Acre	Per Man Hr.	Hours	Man Minutes
Paquito Casas	TH -Flat front yard and inside unit and open back yard	600 SF	36" deck	22 50	1,633	83 50	.27 hr.	16 min.
	TH -Hill in front or enclosed back yard or end unit	600 SF	36" deck	24 80	1,800	82 50	.30	18
	TH -Two of above	780 SF	36" deck	26 80	1,508	81 50	.33	20
	TH -Three of above	780 SF	36" deck	29	1,634	78 50	.37	22
	1/8 acre	5,445 SF	5' deck	29	234	72 50	.40	24
	1/7	6,223 SF	5' deck	30	210	70	.43	26
	1/6	7,260 SF	5' deck	31	186	67 50	.46	28
Mediano Casass	1/5	8,712 SF	6' deck	33	165	65	.51	30
	1/4	10,890 SF	6' deck	35 50	142	62 50	.57	34
	1/3	14,520 SF	6' deck	38 50	120	57 50	.67	40
	1/2	21,780 SF	6' deck	41 80	87	55	.76	46
	3/4	32,670 SF	6' deck	47 25	63	52 50	.90	54
Grande Casas	1	43,560 SF	6' deck	50	50	47 50	1.05	63
	1-1/4		11' deck	54	43 20	46	1.17	70
	1-1/2		11' deck	60	40	45	1.33	80
	1-3/4		11' deck	65	37 15	44	1.48	89
	2		11' deck	70	35	43	1.63	98
	2-1/4		11' deck	76	33 75	42	1.81	109
	2-1/2		11' deck	81	32 40	41	1.98	119
	2-3/4		11' deck	86	31 25	40	2.15	129
	3		11' deck	90	30	40	2.33	140
	3-1/4		11' deck	97	30	40	2.46	148
	3-1/2		11' deck	105	30	40	2.59	155
	3-3/4		11' deck	112	30	40	2.72	163
	4		11' deck	120	30	40	2.85	171
	4-1/4		11' deck	127	30	40	2.97	178
	4-1/2		11' deck	135	30	40	3.10	186
	4-3/4		11' deck	142	30	40	3.23	194
	5 (each extra acre is $30 more)		11' deck	150	30	40	3.33	200

Edging: Prices incl. edging short walk from driveway to front door, no common walk.
For more edging than that, charge .03 L.F. per edging.

○ Basic lawn (Average front & back yards. Approx 5' wide side yards. No common walk.)

For lots requiring extra time:

A. If lot has a common walk, measure both sides of common walk and multiply total by 3¢. Round that total to nearest dollar and add that to per mow price.
B. If lot has a steep slope requiring a walk-behind mower, estimate how much longer it will take to mow, & use right-hand column above to determine price.
C. If lot is heavily treed (an excessive number of trees for a lot that size), estimate how much longer it will take to mow and trim, and use right-hand column above to determine price.
D. If lot has a fence around the back and/or front yard, estimate how much longer it will take to mow and trim, and use right-hand column to determine price.

An Example of a Company's Pricing for Mowing Services

Top Soil
Double Screened

Or **Earthlife**
(Organic compost)

Or **LeafGro**

Effective 5/8/03 Quantity	Installed by CUSTOMER			Installed by				
	Delivered Price Per Cubic Yd.	Total Price	Incl. Tax	Labor Per		Installed Price Per		Total Price
				Bag	Cu. Yd.	Bag	Cu. Yd.	
Bags 1-25				1.50	112.50	4.00	300.00	Depends on Quantity
26-50		Not available		1.25	93.75	3.50	262.50	
51-75				1.00	75.00	3.00	225.00	
Bulk 2 Cu. Yds.	$42.86	$ 85.72	$ 90.00		60		105.00	$210.00
3	35.24	105.72	111.00		60		97.00	291.00
4	29.53	118.12	124.00		57		88.00	352.00
5	28.00	140.00	147.00		55		84.40	422.00
6	27.30	163.80	172.00		52		80.67	484.00
7	27.08	189.56	199.00		50		78.43	549.00
8	27.03	216.24	227.00		49		77.37	619.00
9	27.09	243.81	256.00		48		76.44	688.00
10	"							
11	"							
12	"							
13	"							
14	"							
15	"							
16	"							
20	"							
25	"							
30	"							
35	"							
40	"							

Note: 53—40 lb. bags of Top Soil = 2,100 lbs. = 1 cu. Yard = 100 SF of coverage 3″ deep

Fill Dirt = Same as Top Soil minus $5/cu. yd. (all amounts)

An Example of a Company's Pricing for Delivering and Installing Top Soil

Mulch
Dark Chocolate Brown
Double Shredded Hardwood

Or Playground Chips (Clean)

| Effective 5/8/03 | Installed by CUSTOMER | | | | Installed by ALLSEASONCARE | | |
Quantity	Delivered Price Per Cu. Yd.	Total Price	Incl. Tax (Mulch / Playground Chips)		Labor Per Cu. Yd.	Installed Price Per Cu. Yd.	Total Price
Bags 1–17	Not Available	Not Available	Mulch	Play-ground Chips	($7 per bag) $63.00	($12 per bag) $108.00	Depends On Quantity
Bulk 2 Cu. Yds.	31.43	$ 62.86	66	75	60.00	93.00	$ 186.00
3	24.76	74.29	78	78	58.00	84.00	252.00
4	20.00	80.00	84	92	56.50	77.50	310.00
5	17.52	87.60	92	108	53.60	72.00	360.00
6	17.46	104.76	110.00 (Mulch or Chips)		51.67	70.00	420.00
7	17.42	121.94	128.00		49.71	68.00	476.00
8	17.50	140.00	147.00		49.12	67.50	540.00
9	17.46	157.14	165.00		47.67	66.00	594.00
10	17.43	174.30	183.00		47.70	66.00	660.00
11	17.49	192.39	202.00		47.64	66.00	726.00
12	17.46	209.52	220.00		47.67	66.00	792.00
13	17.44	226.72	238.00		47.69	66.00	858.00
14	17.48	244.72	257.00		47.64	66.00	924.00
15	16.95	254.25	267.00		48.20	66.00	990.00
16	16.97	271.52	285.00		48.19	66.00	1056.00
20	16.95	339.00	356.00		48.20	66.00	1320.00
25	16.99	424.75	446.00		48.16	66.00	1650.00
30	16.99	509.70	535.00		48.16	66.00	1980.00
35	16.98	594.30	624.00		48.17	66.00	2310.00
40	16.98	679.20	713.00		48.17	66.00	2640.00

Note: 9—3 cu. ft. bags of mulch = 1 cu. yd. = 100 SF of coverage 3″ deep

Dyed Mulch = 2 × $

An Example of a Company's Pricing for Delivering and Installing Mulch

Financial Statements

Exterior Installation Contracting

	Exterior Installation Contracting	High Profit Installation	Residential Exterior Installation	Commercial Exterior Installation
BALANCE SHEET				
Assets				
Cash & Marketable Securities	8.8%	11.3%	11.8%	7.1%
Accounts Receivable	37.8	47.5	38.5	38.8
Inventory	9.4	2.2	4.5	9.9
Other Current Assets	4.4	2.3	4.1	5.0
Total Current Assets	60.5	63.3	58.9	60.9
Fixed & Noncurrent Assets	39.5	36.7	41.1	39.1
Total Assets	100.0%	100.0%	100.0%	100.0%
Liabilities and Net Worth				
Accounts Payable	13.9%	12.0%	13.6%	14.8%
Notes Payable	11.5	8.2	11.0	9.2
Other Current Liabilities	6.9	6.8	5.9	9.6
Total Current Liabilities	32.4	27.0	30.5	33.7
Long Term Liabilities	18.6	16.9	19.6	18.0
Net Worth or Owner Equity	49.0	56.0	49.9	48.3
Total Liabilities & Net Worth	100.0%	100.0%	100.0%	100.0%
FINANCIAL RATIOS				
Current Ratio	1.9	2.3	1.9	1.8
Quick Ratio	1.4	2.2	1.6	1.4
Accounts Payable Payout Period (Days)	45.4	48.1	40.3	57.5
Debt To Equity	1.0	0.8	1.0	1.1
EBIT To Total Assets	15.7%	29.0%	14.0%	15.7%
Times Interest Earned	4.7	10.6	3.8	6.9
PRODUCTIVITY RATIOS				
Cash Sales (% Of Net Sales)	0.0%	0.0%	0.5%	0.0%
Average Collection Period (Days)	45.3	50.7	30.8	53.8
Inventory Turnover	14.6	16.4	14.6	14.3
Inventory Holding Period (Days)	24.9	22.3	24.9	25.6
Sales To Fixed Assets	9.7	8.1	10.6	8.7
Number Of Permanent Employees	18	22	11	22
Number Of Seasonal Employees	10	5	6	13
Sales Per Employee	$77,926	$76,851	$68,329	$81,751
Gross Margin Per Employee	$28,032	$27,108	$26,548	$29,762
Payroll Per Employee	$27,835	$22,279	$26,163	$31,002
Payroll Expense (% Of Sales)	39.4%	36.5%	36.7%	40.3%
CASH SUFFICIENCY RATIOS				
Cash Flow Cycle				
Average Collection Period (Days)	45.3	50.7	30.8	53.8
Plus Inventory Holding Period (Days)	24.9	22.3	24.9	25.6
Gross Cash Flow (Days)	70.2	73.0	55.7	79.4
Minus A/P Payout Period (Days)	45.4	48.1	40.3	57.5
Cash Cycle (Days)	24.8	24.9	15.4	21.9
Cash To Current Liabilities	27.1%	41.7%	38.7%	20.9%
Defensive Interval (Days)	20.3	41.6	23.8	17.2
Sales To Working Capital	6.1	6.8	12.5	5.0

A Summary of Exterior Installation Balance Sheet and Ratio Percentage Averages Obtained from a 2000 Landscape Contracting Industry Survey

Source: Operating Cost Study, Professional Landcare Network, Herndon, VA.

Exterior Maintenance

	Exterior Maintenance	High Profit Maintenance	Residential Exterior Maintenance	Commercial Exterior Maintenance
BALANCE SHEET				
Assets				
Cash & Marketable Securities	8.8%	19.4%	13.2%	7.8%
Accounts Receivable	35.3	38.3	26.8	40.9
Inventory	2.4	1.4	1.7	1.6
Other Current Assets	5.3	2.8	3.3	5.9
Total Current Assets	51.8	61.9	45.0	56.3
Fixed & Noncurrent Assets	48.2	38.1	55.0	43.7
Total Assets	100.0%	100.0%	100.0%	100.0%
Liabilities and Net Worth				
Accounts Payable	9.6%	5.2%	8.1%	10.2%
Notes Payable	7.2	5.1	6.3	8.2
Other Current Liabilities	6.3	6.1	8.4	6.1
Total Current Liabilities	23.1	16.5	22.8	24.4
Long Term Liabilities	28.3	15.4	27.5	27.0
Net Worth or Owner Equity	48.6	68.2	49.7	48.6
Total Liabilities & Net Worth	100.0%	100.0%	100.0%	100.0%
FINANCIAL RATIOS				
Current Ratio	2.2	3.8	2.0	2.3
Quick Ratio	1.9	3.5	1.8	2.0
Accounts Payable Payout Period (Days)	64.6	46.0	46.7	76.2
Debt To Equity	1.1	0.5	1.0	1.1
EBIT To Total Assets	19.8%	40.1%	13.2%	20.7%
Times Interest Earned	5.6	18.0	3.8	8.1
PRODUCTIVITY RATIOS				
Cash Sales (% Of Net Sales)	0.0%	0.3%	0.0%	0.0%
Average Collection Period (Days)	36.2	43.5	30.6	41.8
Inventory Turnover	11.5	13.7	11.5	12.3
Inventory Holding Period (Days)	31.8	26.6	31.8	29.6
Sales To Fixed Assets	8.3	8.6	7.1	8.4
Number Of Permanent Employees	25	25	12	30
Number Of Seasonal Employees	20	35	11	29
Sales Per Employee	$62,370	$76,756	$65,593	$59,518
Gross Margin Per Employee	$27,838	$40,937	$25,417	$28,030
Payroll Per Employee	$31,810	$34,053	$31,060	$32,270
Payroll Expense (% Of Sales)	51.1%	49.4%	49.8%	51.2%
CASH SUFFICIENCY RATIOS				
Cash Flow Cycle				
Average Collection Period (Days)	36.2	43.5	30.6	41.8
Plus Inventory Holding Period (Days)	31.8	26.6	31.8	29.6
Gross Cash Flow (Days)	68.0	70.1	62.4	71.4
Minus A/P Payout Period (Days)	64.6	46.0	46.7	76.2
Cash Cycle (Days)	3.4	24.1	15.8	-4.8
Cash To Current Liabilities	37.9%	118.0%	57.8%	32.1%
Defensive Interval (Days)	19.5	60.9	41.1	14.4
Sales To Working Capital	11.8	7.1	12.3	11.6

©2001 Associated Landscape Contractors of America/
American Nursery & Landscape Association

30

A Summary of Exterior Maintenance Balance and Ratio Percentages Obtained from a 2000 Landscape Contracting Industry Survey

Source: Operating Cost Study, Professional Landcare Network, Herndon, VA.

Exterior Installation Contracting

	Exterior Installation Contracting	High Profit Installation	Residential Exterior Installation	Commercial Exterior Installation
Typical Sales Volume	$1,767,035	$1,800,000	$1,330,947	$3,403,371
INCOME STATEMENT				
Net Sales	100.0%	100.0%	100.0%	100.0%
Direct Job Costs				
Direct Labor	23.3	23.1	23.5	23.2
Direct Labor Payroll Taxes (incl. FICA & Unemp.)	2.2	2.0	2.1	2.4
Material Costs (incl. Tax/Freight)	29.9	27.5	28.9	30.8
Subcontractors	5.4	4.6	5.6	4.9
Other Direct Job Costs	0.3	0.2	0.4	0.2
Total Direct Job Costs	**61.0**	**57.3**	**60.5**	**61.5**
Gross Margin	**39.0**	**42.7**	**39.5**	**38.5**
Indirect Overhead				
Indirect Labor	1.9	3.2	0.9	3.2
Replacement Expenses	0.0	0.0	0.0	0.2
Small Tools & Supplies	0.7	0.6	0.8	0.7
Equipment Rental/Lease	1.5	0.9	1.5	1.4
Fuel & Oil	1.9	1.7	2.5	1.7
Equipment/Vehicle Insurance	0.7	0.6	0.7	0.8
Equipment Parts & Repair Expense	2.5	1.8	2.8	2.3
Miscellaneous Indirect Expenses	1.0	0.6	1.4	0.7
Total Indirect Overhead	**10.2**	**9.4**	**10.6**	**10.9**
General & Administrative Overhead				
Advertising & Promotion	0.7	0.6	0.9	0.4
Depreciation	3.7	2.9	3.7	3.6
Insurance—Hospital & Life	1.0	1.0	1.1	1.0
Insurance—Liability	0.6	0.5	0.6	0.7
Insurance—Workers' Compensation	1.0	1.4	1.0	0.9
Office Expense	0.9	0.9	1.0	0.7
Payroll Taxes (incl. FICA & Unemp.)	1.3	0.9	1.6	1.0
Profit Sharing/Pension	0.3	0.2	0.3	0.3
Rent/Facilities	1.6	1.9	1.9	1.2
Salaries—Owners/Officers	6.0	3.4	6.1	5.8
Salaries—Clerical & Administrative	2.4	4.6	2.4	2.5
Salaries—Sales & Commission	1.1	1.0	1.0	1.4
Telephone, Radio, Fax, etc.	0.9	1.1	1.2	0.7
Travel & Entertainment Expense	0.6	0.4	0.7	0.5
Utilities	0.4	0.3	0.4	0.3
Miscellaneous Expenses	1.6	1.3	1.6	1.5
Total General & Admin. Overhead	**23.9**	**22.6**	**25.3**	**22.3**
Operating Profit	**4.8**	**10.7**	**3.6**	**5.3**
Other Income	0.0	0.0	0.0	0.2
Interest Expense	1.0	1.0	1.0	0.8
Other Expenses	0.0	0.1	0.0	0.0
Profit Before Taxes	**3.8%**	**9.7%**	**2.7%**	**4.7%**
Profit Before Taxes + Owners' Salary	**9.8%**	**13.1%**	**8.8%**	**10.5%**

Exterior Installation Income Cost Percentage Averages Obtained from a 2000 Landscape Contracting Industry Survey

Source: Operating Cost Study, Professional Landcare Network, Herndon, VA.

Exterior Maintenance

	Exterior Maintenance	High Profit Maintenance	Residential Exterior Maintenance	Commercial Exterior Maintenance
Typical Sales Volume	$2,210,133	$3,798,414	$1,324,000	$2,985,800
INCOME STATEMENT				
Net Sales	100.0%	100.0%	100.0%	100.0%
Direct Job Costs				
Direct Labor	28.6	26.0	27.4	29.0
Direct Labor Payroll Taxes (incl. FICA & Unemp.)	3.3	2.8	3.2	3.1
Material Costs (incl. Tax/Freight)	15.5	12.2	18.9	14.1
Subcontractors	5.0	6.4	3.8	5.8
Other Direct Job Costs	0.8	0.6	0.3	0.9
Total Direct Job Costs	53.1	48.1	53.6	52.9
Gross Margin	46.9	51.9	46.4	47.1
Indirect Overhead				
Indirect Labor	4.9	4.6	3.3	5.0
Replacement Expenses	0.2	0.0	0.2	0.1
Small Tools & Supplies	0.9	0.8	1.0	0.8
Equipment Rental/Lease	1.3	0.9	0.7	1.4
Fuel & Oil	2.6	2.5	2.3	2.5
Equipment/Vehicle Insurance	0.7	0.6	0.9	0.6
Equipment Parts & Repair Expense	3.0	3.2	3.4	2.7
Miscellaneous Indirect Expenses	1.1	0.8	0.8	0.9
Total Indirect Overhead	14.8	13.4	12.3	14.1
General & Administrative Overhead				
Advertising & Promotion	0.7	0.4	1.2	0.6
Depreciation	3.3	3.7	4.8	3.3
Insurance—Hospital & Life	1.2	1.1	1.5	1.2
Insurance—Liability	0.7	0.8	0.6	0.7
Insurance—Workers' Compensation	1.0	1.1	1.0	1.0
Office Expense	1.1	0.8	1.3	0.9
Payroll Taxes (incl. FICA & Unemp.)	1.1	1.0	1.4	1.1
Profit Sharing/Pension	0.3	0.5	0.4	0.3
Rent/Facilities	2.0	1.5	2.3	2.0
Salaries—Owners/Officers	5.3	5.7	6.4	5.6
Salaries—Clerical & Administrative	4.7	5.0	4.2	5.0
Salaries—Sales & Commission	1.3	1.0	0.9	1.5
Telephone, Radio, Fax, etc.	1.1	0.9	1.2	1.0
Travel & Entertainment Expense	0.4	0.3	0.5	0.4
Utilities	0.3	0.3	0.5	0.3
Miscellaneous Expenses	2.2	1.9	2.0	2.6
Total General & Admin. Overhead	26.7	26.0	30.3	27.6
Operating Profit	5.4	12.5	3.8	5.4
Other Income	0.2	0.2	0.2	0.4
Interest Expense	1.0	0.7	1.1	0.7
Other Expenses	0.0	0.0	0.0	0.0
Profit Before Taxes	4.6%	12.0%	3.0%	5.1%
Profit Before Taxes + Owners' Salary	9.9%	17.8%	9.4%	10.6%

Exterior Maintenance Income Cost Percentage Averages Obtained from a 2000 Landscape Contracting Industry Survey

Source: Operating Cost Study, Professional Landcare Network, Herndon, VA.

Index

191